USING PRIMARY SOURCES TO TEAC

THE AMERICAN CIVIL WAR

MEN OF COLOR
TO ARMS! TO ARMS!
NOW OR NEVER

This is our golden moment! The Government of the United States calls for every Able-bodied Colored Man to enter the Army for the

Three Years' Service!

FAIL NOW, & OUR RACE IS DOOMED

THE POLITICAL QUADRILLE
Music by Dred Scott

TERRIFIC COMBAT BETWEEN THE "MONITOR" 2 GUNS & "MERRIMAC" 10 GUNS.

Written by Rebecca Stark

ISBN 978-1-56644-616-7

EDUCATIONAL BOOKS 'N' BINGO

Printed in the United States of America.

Table of Contents

Using Primary Sources in the Classroom

Primary sources are original materials from the past. They comprise birth certificates, legal documents, speeches, letters, diary entries, ledgers, political cartoons, posters, advertisements, stamps, photographs, maps, newspaper articles, and other first-hand records. Primary sources help us to understand the period in which they were created and to gain insight into the people of that period.

The study of primary sources engages students in active learning and encourages higher-level thinking. Students are given opportunities to use their inferencing skills to interpret the documents and other items they analyze. They also use important application, analysis, and evaluation skills. By examining a variety of documents on the same topic, students develop an understanding that people interpret events from differing points of view.

Another benefit that can be derived from the study of primary sources is that students often rethink preconceived notions about people and events. They come to realize that their biases and prejudices may be based upon faulty information. By learning how people from the past felt, they often develop empathy for those people.

ABOUT THIS BOOK

Background material regarding the subject is provided. Following this information are Think About It activities, which present challenging activities to promote critical thinking.

All documents and excerpts, including their transcriptions, retain the original spellings and grammar.

Comprehensive answers are provided in the Answer Section.

Document Analysis Worksheets are provided for a few types of primary-source materials. These worksheets were designed and developed by the Education Staff, National Archives and Records Administration, Washington, DC, 20408. You will find them at the end of this resource.

SUGGESTIONS

Vocabulary
Instruct students to make a list of unfamiliar vocabulary as they read. Encourage them to use context clues to figure out the meanings of words they do not know and to look up the definition if they are not sure about a meaning. Help students as needed with difficult spellings in the original documents.

Images
Have the students find color versions of some of the images online if appropriate. Elicit from them how seeing them in color enhanced the experience.

**The use of primary sources in your classroom can bring
history to life for you and your students. Enjoy the journey!**

The American Civil War
Background Information

Also known as the War Between the States, the American Civil War was fought from 1861 to 1865. The factors that led to the conflict had been brewing for decades. Most stemmed from the fact that the North and the South had very different economies. The North's economy was based on manufacturing and industry. The South's was based on the large-scale farming of the plantations. Those plantations depended upon slave labor, especially for their two main cash crops: tobacco and cotton.

With westward expansion and the spread of slavery into those new territories, abolitionist sentiment in the North grew. When Abraham Lincoln was elected President in 1860, Southerners feared that slavery in America would come to an end. Even before he took office, therefore, seven states seceded from the Union and declared that they were forming a new Confederate States of America. When Confederate soldiers fired on Fort Sumter on April 12, 1861, the War Between the States officially began. By June 8 of that year, eleven states had seceded from the Union and joined the Confederacy.

When the conflict ended about four years later, more than 600,000 soldiers from both the North and the South would have died, and much of the South would be left in ruin.

The Missouri Compromise of 1820—When Missouri petitioned for admission to the Union as a slave state, a compromise was reached. Missouri would enter as a slave state; Maine would enter as a free state; and, with the exception of Missouri, slavery would be prohibited north of the 36° 30' parallel.

Compromise of 1850—The Compromise of 1850 comprised five laws based on resolutions introduced by Senator Henry Clay. The laws dealt with the issue of slavery and were an attempt to avoid a crisis between the North and the South and to keep the Union together.

Fugitive Slave Law of 1850—The first Fugitive Slave Act, which was passed in 1793, required all states to forcibly return slaves who had escaped from other states to their original owners. By the mid-1800s, Northern states were refusing to abide by that law. The Fugitive Slave Act of 1850 was passed as part of the Compromise of 1850 between Southerners with slave-holding interests and Northerners who opposed the expansion of slavery into the Western territories.

The Kansas-Nebraska Act of 1854—This act provided that the populations living in territories could decide for themselves whether to be slave or free. It repealed the Missouri Compromise of 1820.

Dred Scott Decision—The Dred Scott Decision was the 7-2 Supreme Court ruling in the legal case known as *Scott v. Sandford*. In its 1857 landmark decision, the Court ruled that African-Americans could not be citizens. It also ruled that Congress could not prohibit slavery in the territories.

Northern Economy—The economy at the start of the Civil War was more diverse in the North than in the South. The Northern economy was based mainly on manufacturing, but banking and trade were also important.

Southern Economy—At the start of the war, the South's economy was booming; this was due in great part to their most important cash crops: tobacco, cotton, and sugar cane. The large farms known as plantations had become the backbone of this economy, and those plantations depended upon a large, cheap source of labor. The Southern planters filled that need with slave labor.

Tariffs—Tariffs are taxes imposed by a government on goods and services imported from other countries. Northerners favored tariffs on goods imported from other nations because tariffs made foreign goods more expensive and, therefore, less competitive. Southerners, who had little manufacturing, wanted imported goods.

"Slave Auction at Richmond, Virginia"—With the growth of plantations and their reliance on slaves came the growth of a new industry—the slave auction.

The Election of 1860—The election of 1860 was an important moment in U.S. history. Although Lincoln did not campaign on a desire to abolish slavery, Southerners knew that he had in the past introduced antislavery legislation and they feared his election would lead to abolition.

Secession—On December 20, 1860, South Carolina seceded from the Union. Eventually eleven Southern slave states seceded. In order of secession they were South Carolina, Mississippi, Florida, Alabama, Georgia, Louisiana, Texas, Virginia, North Carolina, Arkansas, and Tennessee. Four border slave states did not secede: Missouri, Kentucky, Maryland, and Delaware. The western portion of Virginia broke away from the rest of the state and formed West Virginia, which became part of the Union in 1863.

Fort Sumter—On April 10, 1861, the Confederates tried to convince the Union to give up its stronghold on Fort Sumter in Charleston Harbor. When negotiations failed, the Confederates decided that force was necessary. Early in the morning on April 12, 1861, they bombarded the fort. On April 13, the Union commander surrendered, and the next day he and his men evacuated the fort.

Jefferson Davis—Jefferson Davis had represented Mississippi in both the Senate and the House of Representatives. He also served as Secretary of War under President Pierce; nevertheless, when Mississippi seceded, he switched loyalties and accepted the position as President of the Confederate States of America.

First Battle of Bull Run—Called the First Battle of Manassas by the Confederates, this was the first major battle of the war. Union forces attacked the Confederates at Manassas Junction, Virginia, in an attempt to open the way to Richmond. The Union troops were forced to retreat. Both sides were surprised by the loss of life and came to the realization that the war would be longer and bloodier than they had thought.

Civil War Espionage—Both the Union and the Confederacy utilized spies during the American Civil War. Rose O'Neal Greenhow was the leader of a well-known Confederate spy ring.

Ironclads—The Battle of Hampton Roads, Virginia, between the *Monitor* and the *Merrimac* on March 9, 1862, marked the beginning of ironclad warfare in the American Civil War.

West Virginia Becomes a State—West Virginia entered the Union on July 4, 1863, as the nation's 35th state after separating from the state of Virginia.

The Battle of Antietam—The bloodiest one-day battle of the American Civil War took place on September 17, 1862, in Sharpsburg, Maryland, along a creek called Antietam.

Clara Barton—Clara Barton was a nurse during the American Civil War. She is best known for founding the American Red Cross.

The Emancipation Proclamation—This proclamation freed the slaves in states in rebellion against the United States of America.

Recruitment Posters—Recruitment posters were valuable tools to entice men to enlist.

Black Soldiers—By the end of the Civil War, about 179,000 black men served as soldiers in the U.S. Army; this was approximately 10% of the Union Army. Another 19,000 served in the Navy.

The Siege of Vicksburg—The Union campaign against Vicksburg, Mississippi, from May 18, 1863, to July 4, 1863, divided the Confederacy. It also reinforced Grant's reputation as a great strategist.

The Battle of Gettysburg—This three-day battle was the bloodiest battle of the American Civil War and is considered a turning point of the conflict.

The Gettysburg Address—President Lincoln delivered this speech at the dedication of the Soldiers' National Cemetery in Gettysburg, Pennsylvania, on Thursday, November 19, 1863.

The Election of 1864—In 1864 President Lincoln ran for re-election. His running mate was Andrew Johnson. Their party was the National Union Party, the temporary name for the Republican Party during the war. They won the election.

General Sherman's March to the Sea—Led by Major General William Tecumseh Sherman, the March to the Sea was a military campaign from Atlanta, Georgia, to Savannah, Georgia. It lasted from November 15 to December 21, 1864.

Mary Edwards Walker: Congressional Medal of Honor—Mary Edwards Walker earned the Medal of Honor for service during the Civil War; she was the first (and as of the writing the only) woman to receive that honor.

The Fall of Richmond—Richmond was the capital of both the state of Virginia and the Confederate States of America. It was also the most important industrial center of the Confederacy. On April 3, 1865, General Grant's Union Army finally took the city.

Surrender at Appomattox Court House—On April 9, 1865, the Army of Northern Virginia, led by General Robert E. Lee, surrendered to General Ulysses S. Grant.

Andersonville Prison—Originally called Camp Sumter, this Confederate prisoner-of-war camp in Georgia is known for the mistreatment of its prisoners. More than 45,000 men were imprisoned here during the last fourteen months of the war, and almost 13,000 of them died while being held here.

Lincoln's Assassination—President Abraham Lincoln was assassinated by John Wilkes Booth, well-known stage actor, on April 14, 1865.

Civil War Music—Music played a very important role for both sides during the American Civil War.

Reconstruction Amendments—The thirteenth, fourteenth, and fifteenth amendments were added during the Reconstruction Era.

The Missouri Compromise

Background Information

By 1819 Missouri's population was large enough for it to apply for statehood. Friction between the antislavery and pro-slavery factions had grown, and the prospect of Missouri's entrance to the Union as a slave state had become more controversial than had once been expected.

When Missouri applied for admission in December 1819, there were eleven slave states and eleven free states. With the admission of Missouri as a slave state, that balance of power would end. A passionate debate followed. Northerners, led by Senator Rufus King of New York, spoke out against allowing slavery in Missouri because it meant the expansion of slavery into the territory acquired as a result of the Louisiana Purchase. Senator William Pinkney of Maryland and other Southerners argued that new states should have the same freedom of choice as the original states.

Eventually a compromise bill was proposed. To maintain the balance of power, Missouri would enter as a slave state, and Maine would enter as a free state. In addition, slavery would be prohibited in all lands obtained as a result of the Louisiana Purchase north of the 36° 30' parallel with the exception of Missouri.

The Missouri Compromise was signed by President James Monroe on March 6, 1820.

Transcript of the Statute Admitting Maine to the Union

STATUTE I.
March 3, 1820
Act of April 7, 1820, ch. 39.
The people of Maine, with the consent of the legislature of Massachusetts, have formed themselves into an independent state, &c.
Maine admitted into the Union from 15th March, 1820.
CHAP. XIX. *An Act for the admission of the state of Maine into the Union. (s)*

WHEREAS, by an act of the state of Massachusetts, passed on the nineteenth day of June, in the year one thousand eight hundred and nineteen, entitled "An act relating to the separation of the district of Maine from Massachusetts proper, and forming the same into a separate and independent state," the people of that part of Massachusetts heretofore known as the district of Maine, did, with the consent of the legislature of said state of Massachusetts, form themselves into an independent state, and did establish a constitution for the government of the same, agreeably to the provisions of said act—Therefore,

Be it enacted by the Senate and House of Representatives of the United States of America, in Congress assembled, That from and after the fifteenth day of March, in the year one thousand eight hundred and twenty, the state of Maine is hereby declared to be one of the United States of America, and admitted into the Union on an equal footing with the original states, in all respects whatever.

Approved, March 3, 1820.

Transcript of Excerpts of the Missouri Compromise (1820)

An Act to authorize the people of the Missouri territory to form a constitution and state government, and for the admission of such state into the Union on an equal footing with the original states, and to prohibit slavery in certain territories.

Be it enacted by the Senate and House of Representatives of the United States of America, in Congress assembled, That the inhabitants of that portion of the Missouri territory included within the boundaries herein after designated, be, and they are hereby, authorized to form for themselves a constitution and state government, and to assume such name as they shall deem proper; and the said state, when formed, shall be admitted into the Union, upon an equal footing with the original states, in all respects whatsoever.

…

SEC. 8. And be it further enacted. That in all that territory ceded by France to the United States, under the name of Louisiana, which lies north of thirty-six degrees and thirty minutes north latitude, not included within the limits of the state, contemplated by this act, slavery and involuntary servitude, otherwise than in the punishment of crimes, whereof the parties shall have been duly convicted, shall be, and is hereby, forever prohibited: Provided always, That any person escaping into the same, from whom labour or service is lawfully claimed, in any state or territory of the United States, such fugitive may be lawfully reclaimed and conveyed to the person claiming his or her labour or service as aforesaid.

APPROVED, March 6, 1820.

Think About It

1. What did Maine have to do before it could be admitted to the Union? Why?

2. What portion of the excerpt shows that Missouri retained the right to have slavery when it was admitted to the Union as a state?

3. What portion of the excerpt prohibited slavery in most areas ceded by France to the United States as part of the Louisiana Purchase? Underline the words that explain the exception.

4. What portion upheld the Fugitive Slave Act?

Excerpts from Thomas Jefferson's April 22, 1820, Letter to James Holmes

I thank you, Dear Sir, for the copy you have been so kind as to send me of the letter to your constituents on the Missouri question. It is a perfect justification to them. I had for a long time ceased to read the newspapers or pay any attention to public affairs, confident they were in good hands, and content to be a passenger in our bark to the shore from which I am not distant. But this momentous question, like a fire bell in the night, awakened and filled me with terror. I considered it at once as the knell of the Union. It is hushed indeed for the moment. But this is a reprieve only, not a final sentence. A geographical line, coinciding with a marked principle, moral and political, once conceived and held up to the angry passions of men, will never be obliterated; and every new irritation will mark it deeper and deeper. I can say with conscious truth that there is not a man on earth who would sacrifice more than I would, to relieve us from this heavy reproach, in any practicable way. The cession of that kind of property, for so it is misnamed, is a bagatelle which would not cost me in a second thought, if, in that way, a general emancipation and expatriation could be effected: and, gradually, and with due sacrifices, I think it might be. But, as it is, we have the wolf by the ear, and we can neither hold him, nor safely let him go. Justice is in one scale, and self-preservation in the other.

…

I regret that I am now to die in the belief that the useless sacrifice of themselves, by the generation of '76, to acquire self government and happiness to their country, is to be thrown away by the unwise and unworthy passions of their sons, and that my only consolation is to be that I live not to weep over it. If they would but dispassionately weigh the blessings they will throw away against an abstract principle more likely to be effected by union than by scission, they would pause before they would perpetrate this act of suicide on themselves and of treason against the hopes of the world.

To yourself as the faithful advocate of union I tender the offering of my high esteem and respect.

Th. Jefferson

Think About It

1. To what was Jefferson referring when he wrote the following: "..this momentous question, like a fire bell in the night, awakened and filled me with terror. I considered it at once as the knell of the Union"?

2. What aspect of the tensions bothered Jefferson the most?

3. Explain Jefferson's use of the idiom "to have a wolf by an ear" in the following excerpt: "But, as it is, we have the wolf by the ear, and we can neither hold him, nor safely let him go. Justice is in one scale, and self-preservation in the other. "

4. Judge Jefferson's view that the Missouri Compromise was "a reprieve only, not a final sentence."

5. How did Jefferson view the generation then in power?

The Compromise of 1850

Background Information

The Compromise of 1850 comprised five laws based on resolutions introduced by Senator Henry Clay, who became known as the " Great Compromiser." The laws dealt with the issue of slavery; they were an attempt to avoid a war between the North and the South and to keep the Union together by considering the interests of the North, the South, and the West.

Terms of the Compromise:

- the Fugitive Slave Act was amended;
- the slave trade in Washington, DC, was abolished;
- California would enter the Union as a free state;
- Utah would be run under a territorial government;
- the boundary dispute between Texas and New Mexico was settled; and
- a territorial government would be established in New Mexico.

Arguments for and against the Compromise were presented in the Senate. Daniel Webster, who at an earlier time argued against the morality of slavery, became a strong advocate for the Compromise. Above all he wanted to keep the Union together and avert war. For that reason, he warned Southerners against secession and Northerners against antislavery measures. John C. Calhoun opposed passage because it limited expansion of slavery into the western territories. Clay, Webster, and Calhoun became known as the "Great Triumvirate."

Henry Clay
Daguerreotype by Julian Vannerson

Daniel Webster
Unknown Artist

John C. Calhoun
Portrait by George P. A. Healy

Think About It

1. Can you find Clay, Webster, and Calhoun in the image entitled "The United States Senate, A.D. 1850" on the next page?

2. Whom does Clay seem to be addressing? How do you know?

"The United States Senate, A.D. 1850"
Drawn by Peter F. Rothermel / Engraved by Robert Whitechurch
Source: Library of Congress

Ralph Waldo Emerson

"If you put a chain around the neck of a slave, the other end fastens itself around your own."
—Ralph Waldo Emerson

The following two poems about Daniel Webster were written by Ralph Waldo Emerson.

1831
Let Webster's lofty face
Ever on thousands shine,
A beacon set that Freedom's race
Might gather omens from that radiant sign.

1854
Why did all manly gifts in Webster fail?
He wrote on Nature's grandest brow, For Sale.

Think About It

1. Analyze the Ralph Waldo Emerson's quotation about slavery.

2. How did Emerson's views of Webster change? Why?

The Fugitive Slave Law of 1850

Background Information

The first Fugitive Slave Act was passed in 1793. It required all states, including those forbidding slavery, to forcibly return slaves who had escaped from other states to their original owners. As Northern states abolished slavery, however, they stopped enforcing the law; some even passed laws making it illegal for state officials to aid in the capture of fugitive slaves.

As part of the Compromise of 1850, the Fugitive Slave Act was amended, and the slave trade in Washington, DC, was abolished. On March 7, 1850, United States nationalist and statesman Daniel Webster delivered a three-hour speech on the issue of states' rights to permit slavery. Five months later, Congress approved the Compromise of 1850 in order to preserve the Union. The Fugitive Slave Act of 1850 was part of that measure.

Daniel Webster Giving States' Rights Speech
Source: Library of Congress

"Practical Illustration of the Fugitive Slave Law"

The political cartoon on the following page satirizes the antagonism between Northern abolitionists and those who supported enforcement of the Fugitive Slave Act of 1850. The abolitionists are represented by William Lloyd Garrison, shown on the left. Secretary of State Daniel Webster, who criticized abolitionists, is shown on his hands and knees.

Written in small print (difficult to see):

Garrison (with arm around woman's waist): "Don't be alarmed Susanna, you're safe enough."

Black man with whip: "It's my turn now Old Slave Driver."

Slave catcher: "Don't back out Webster, if you do we're ruind."

Webster, holding the Constitution: "This, though Constitutional, is 'extremely disagreeable.'"

Man (second from the right) holding volumes of *Law & Gospel* under his arms: "We will give these fellows a touch of South Carolina."

Man with quill and ledger: "I goes in for Law & Order."

A fallen slaveholder: "This is all 'your' fault Webster."

A day, an hour of virtuous Liberty, is worth an age of Servitude   TEMPLE OF LIBERTY   All men are born free & equal

PRACTICAL ILLUSTRATION OF THE FUGITIVE SLAVE LAW.

Source: Library of Congress

Think About It

1. Garrison is pointing his gun at the man on Webster's back. Who, do you think, is that man? How do you know?

2. Webster is holding a copy of the Constitution. Based upon this cartoon, how do you think Webster felt about enforcing the Fugitive Slave Law?

3. On which side do you think the artist was? Cite examples.

4. The fallen slaveholder blames Webster for his downfall. Why might he have been to blame?

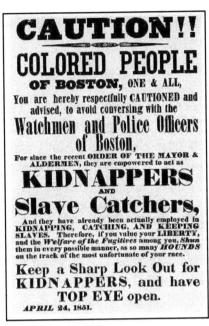

Think About It: "Caution!! Colored People of Boston"

1. What was the purpose of this broadside?

2. Why was the warning necessary?

3. What is the date on the poster? What is the significance of this date?

"What's Sauce for the Goose Is Sauce for the Gander"

The left panel of the cartoon by Edward Williams Clay illustrates the abolitionist's invocation of a "higher law" against the claim of a slave owner: " 'What! seize my African brother! never! I dont recognize any U.S. law! I have a higher law, a law of my own....' " On the counter is a copy of the newspaper the *Emancipator Palmetto*. The right panel depicts a Northerner who claims that several bolts of fabric have been stolen from him. The slaveholder asks, "They are fugitives from you, are they?" He then states, "As to the law of the land, I have a higher law of my own, and possession is nine points in the law."

Think About It

1. Do you think Clay was for or against the Fugitive Slave Act?

2. Explain the meaning of the cartoon's title.

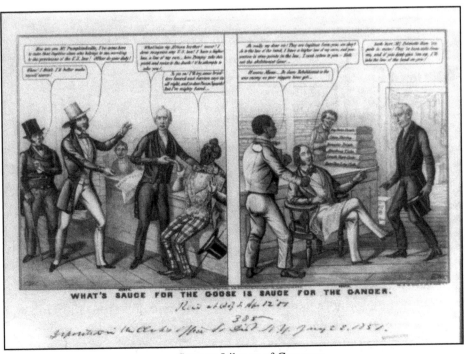

Source: Library of Congress

The Kansas-Nebraska Act

Background Information

The Kansas-Nebraska Act was proposed by Democratic Senator Stephen A. Douglas of Illinois. He wanted to build a transcontinental railroad that would cross Chicago. As part of his plan, he hoped to increase the population along the way by opening up new farms in Nebraska. However, the only way farmers would be able to claim the land was if the land was part of an organized territory. For that reason settlers would not move to Nebraska unless the area became a territory. Southern representatives in Congress did not want Nebraska to become a territory because the land lay north of the 36°30' parallel; slavery was prohibited there because of the Missouri Compromise.

To appease the Southerners, Douglas proposed a bill that would organize both Kansas and Nebraska. It was based on a principle that became known as "popular sovereignty." Simply put, territories would decide the issue of slavery for themselves based upon a popular vote. Southerners thought that even though Kansas was below the 36° 30' parallel, it was next to Missouri, a slave state, and might vote against abolition. Although opposition was strong, the Kansas-Nebraska Act passed in May 1854.

Passage of this act led to many conflicts between pro-slavery and antislavery factions. In fact, the period of extreme violence that followed became known as Bleeding Kansas.

Think About It

1. How did the passage of this act affect the Missouri Compromise?

2. This act caused a rush into Kansas Territory. Why?

"Southern Chivalry"

On May 19 and 20 of 1856 Senator Charles Sumner of Massachusetts addressed the Senate. In his two-day speech, which is commonly called "The Crime Against Kansas," he spoke against the violence that was occurring in Kansas as a result of the Kansas-Nebraska Act. His antislavery speech was especially harsh against Senator Andrew Butler of South Carolina.

Senator Butler's cousin, Representative Preston Brooks, was furious. His first thought was to challenge Sumner to a duel, but he knew that Sumner would not accept. Instead Brooks confronted Sumner on the floor of the U.S. Senate on May 22 and beat him viciously with a gold-handled cane.

Sumner was seriously injured both mentally and physically, but Brooks was never punished. Although the Northerners tried to have him expelled from the House, the Southerners prevented them from getting the necessary two-thirds majority. Brooks resigned, but then won unanimously when a special election was held to fill the vacancy.

SOUTHERN CHIVALRY — ARGUMENT versus CLUB'S.

Political Cartoon by Artist John L. Magee, 1856

Think About It

1. The above political cartoon appeared in a newspaper. Do you think it was a Northern paper or a Southern one?

2. In what way did the artist show Sumner in a positive light?

3. In general, what do you think was the point of view of the artist?

4. What do you notice about the senators in the background?

The Dred Scott Decision

Background Information

Dred Scott was a slave who had moved with his owner, John Emerson, from Missouri to Illinois and then to Wisconsin Territory. Missouri was a slave state, but Illinois was a free state, and Wisconsin Territory was a free territory. When Emerson died, Scott tried to buy his freedom from Emerson's widow, but she refused. In 1846 antislavery attorneys helped Dred Scott and his wife Harriet file a lawsuit in a Missouri state court. The grounds for their suit was that their residence in Illinois and Wisconsin Territory had freed them. Dred's case went forward, and in 1850 the Missouri court declared him a free man. Two years later, however, Mrs. Emerson appealed the decision and the Missouri Supreme Court reversed that verdict. The doctrine "once free, always free" ended.

Photographer Unknown, c. 1857

Mrs. Emerson gave control of her late husband's estate to her brother, John F.A. Sanford (later incorrectly spelled Sandford). Because Sanford was a New York state resident, Scott couldn't sue in Missouri; therefore, Scott's attorneys filed their lawsuit in a federal court. Eventually, the case went to the U.S. Supreme Court.

In March 1857 the landmark decision now known as the Dred Scott Decision was announced. The Court ruled 7-2 against Dred Scott. Chief Justice Roger Brooke Taney wrote the majority opinion.

Taney used the case to proclaim that Congress had no right to prohibit or abolish slavery in the territories and that the Missouri Compromise was unconstitutional. Regarding Scott's status, Taney ruled that in spite of his residence in Illinois, Scott was not free because he had re-entered Missouri. A few years later the Blow family, who had sold Scott to Emerson, bought Dred Scott and his wife Harriet and set them free. Ten years after Dred Scott first sued for his freedom, he was a free man.

Think About It

1. In your opinion, why did Mrs. Emerson appeal the decision to grant Dred Scott freedom?

2. How would you describe Dred Scott's actions?

Transcription of Points 4 through 9 of the Dred Scott Decision

4. A free negro of the African race, whose ancestors were brought to this country and sold as slaves, is not a "citizen" within the meaning of the Constitution of the United States.

5. When the Constitution was adopted, they were not regarded in any of the States as members of the community which constituted the State, and were not numbered among its "people or citizen." Consequently, the special rights and immunities guarantied to citizens do not apply to them. And not being "citizens" within the meaning of the Constitution, they are not entitled to sue in that character in a court of the United States, and the Circuit Court has not jurisdiction in such a suit.

6. The only two clauses in the Constitution which point to this race, treat them as persons whom it was morally lawful to deal in as articles of property and to hold as slaves.

7. Since the adoption of the Constitution of the United States, no state can by any subsequent law make a foreigner or any other description of persons citizens of the United States, nor entitle them to the rights and privileges secured to citizens by that instrument.

8. A State, by its laws passed since the adoption of the Constitution, may put a foreigner or any other description of persons upon a footing with its own citizens, as to all the rights and privileges enjoyed by them within its dominion, and by its laws. But that will not make him a citizen of the United States, nor entitle him to sue in its courts, nor to any of the privileges and immunities of a citizen in another State.

9. The change in public opinion and feeling in relation to the African race, which has taken place since the adoption of the Constitution, cannot change its construction and meaning, and it must be construct and administered now according to its true meaning and intention when it was formed and adopted.

3. On what basis did Dred Scott sue for his freedom?

4. On what basis did the Supreme Court rule against him?

The Northern Economy

Background Information

Although most people still lived on farms, the economy at the start of the Civil War was much more diverse in the North than in the South. The Northern economy was based mainly on manufacturing, but banking and trade were also important.

Factories and the Growth of Cities

An important reason for the growth of factories was the increase in the production of cotton after the invention of the cotton gin. Much of that cotton was exported to the Northern states to be made into cloth. Before the Industrial Revolution, most things were made by hand. Eventually the development of advanced machinery made many different types of factories possible. Textiles were the most important industry in terms of employment, but other industries also gained importance; among them were steel, oil, lumber, iron foundries, and flour milling.

Unlike in the South, where planters relied on slave labor, Northern factory owners depended upon wage earners. Workers migrated to the centers of trade, where work was available. This resulted in the rise of new industrial cities. Many of those who migrated to the cities were immigrants; they provided an ample supply of cheap labor. As a result, a new class of wealthy businessmen developed. These men amassed large fortunes and became known as the "captains of industry."

Power Looms

The invention of the power loom was an important factor in the growth of textile mills in the North. Although Francis Cabot Lowell did not invent the power loom, he was responsible for bringing improvements to the manufacture of power looms to the United States.

The Industrial Revolution in Britain was more advanced than in the United States. While visiting factories in Great Britain in 1811, Lowell memorized the designs and workings of the power looms he saw there. Together with master mechanic Paul Moody, he used the knowledge gained in Great Britain to develop a similar system in Massachusetts.

Canals and Railroads

Most canals and railroads were in the North.

- The Erie Canal was completed in 1825; it connected Lake Erie with the Hudson River.
- Construction on the first railroad, the Baltimore & Ohio, began in 1828; the first section opened in 1830.

On the next page is an advertisement for the Baltimore and Ohio Railroad. It was originally on page 52 of *Wood's Baltimore City Directory for 1864*. The following is an excerpt:

The well-earned reputation of this Road for SPEED, SECURITY and COMFORT will be more than sustained.... In addition to the *Unequalled Attractions of Natural Scenery* heretofore conceded to this route, *the recent Troubles upon the Border* have associated numerous points on the Road, between the Ohio River and Harper's Ferry with painful but instructive interest.

Think About It

1. What was the main purpose of this ad? What specific important information did the ad give to customers?

2. According to the poster, why did the railroad have a good reputation? What past benefit of the route would still be there? What was the new benefit of the route?

3. Which side controlled the railroad? How do you know?

4. What city could be visited for an extra charge?

5. Where did the damage that forced the railroad to close occur? Research to find out who was responsible.

Using Primary Sources to Teach U.S. History: The American Civil War

Lowell Mills Boarding Houses

Lowell recruited a specific type of worker for his textile mills: single girls aged fifteen to thirty-five. These girls signed a contract with provisions stating that they agreed to do the following:

- to work in the factory at least one year;
- to live in a company boarding house; and
- to attend church regularly.

Lowell's early boarding houses were wooden structures, but as the company grew, rows of brick boarding houses were constructed adjacent to his mills.

Think About It

1. Read the letter on the next page. When did Mary Paul write it?

2. What did you learn about the working conditions of the mill from reading the letter? Give examples.

3. What portion of Mary's salary went toward her boarding-house rent?

4. How many hours a day did Mary typically work?

5. How did Mary feel about her job?

6. Most of the girls who worked in the Lowell Mills were between 15 and 25. How do you think you would feel if you had to live in a company boarding house and work in the mill?

A Lowell Boarding House
Source: Library of Congress

© **Barbara M. Peller**

A Letter Home

The following is the transcript of a letter written by Mary Paul, a worker in one of the Lowell Mills factories, to her father.

Lowell, Dec 21st 1845

Dear Father,

I received your letter on Thursday the 14th with much pleasure. I am well which is one comfort. My life and health are spared while others are cut off. Last Thursday one girl fell down and broke her neck which caused instant death. She was going in or coming out of the mill and slipped down it being very icy, the same day as a man was killed by the cars, another had nearly all of his ribs broken, another was nearly killed by falling down and having a bale of cotton fall on him. Last Tuesday we were paid. In all I had six dollars and sixty cents paid $4.68 for board, with the rest I got me a pair of rubbers and a pair of 50 cts shoes. Next payment I am to have a dollar a week besides my board. We have not had much snow, the deepest being not more than 4 inches. It has been very warm for winter. Perhaps you would like something about our regulations about going in and coming out of the mill. At 5 o'clock in the morning the bell rings for the folks to get up and get breakfast. At half past six it rings for the girls to get up and at seven they are called into the mill. At half past 12 we have dinner are called back again at one and stay till half past seven. I get along very well with my work. I can doff as fast as any girl in our room. I think I shall have frames before long. The usual time allowed for learning is six months but I think I shall have frames before I have been in three as long as I get along so fast. I think that the factory is the best place for me and if any girl wants employment I advise them to come to Lowell. Tell Harriet that although she does not hear from me she is not forgotten. I have so little time to devote to writing that I cannot write all I want to. There are half a dozen letters which I ought to write to day but I have not time. Tell Harriet I send my love to her and all of the girls. Give my love to Mrs. Clement. Tell Henry this will answer for him and you too for this time.

This from
Mary Paul

Bela Paul
S. Henry Paul

Source: "The Paul Family Papers, Vermont Historical Society."

The Southern Economy

Background Information

Just before the war began, most of the nation worked on farms, but the economies of the North and the South differed greatly. The economy of the South was based upon its cash crops: tobacco, cotton, rice, sugar cane, and indigo. By the mid-1800s, cotton had taken over as its most profitable crop. This was due in great part to the invention of the cotton gin.

By the start of the war in 1861, the United States was producing 75% of the world's supply of cotton, and the South was responsible for 75% of that production. Most was either exported to Europe or shipped to the textile mills of New England.

Invention of the Cotton Gin

The most tedious part of growing, picking, and preparing cotton was picking out the tiny seeds from the cotton plant by hand. Picking out the seeds from long-staple cotton wasn't too tedious, but it only grew along the coast. Removing them from short-staple cotton was very time consuming.

Early cotton gins could be used only with the long-staple cotton. Eli Whitney's cotton gin, however, could be used with short-staple cotton. For this reason, his invention had a significant effect on the rise in cotton production. He patented his invention in 1794. Unfortunately, many copied his device without paying him a royalty. This was possible because of a loophole in the Patent Act of 1793. The law was amended in 1800, but it was too late for Whitney to profit from his invention.

Plantations

The large increase in the production of cotton led to the growth of large farms known as plantations.

Culture in the South basically revolved around plantation life. Plantations were self-sufficient. In fact, many were like small towns. The growth of plantations, in turn, led to an increase in slavery. They relied on slave labor, and slaves became the wealthy planters' most valuable investments.

The image on the right is of a Currier & Ives print. Although it was done in 1884, it presents a good representation of life on a Southern plantation.

Cotton plantation on the Mississippi, 1884
Source: Library of Congress

The following is the url to view the print in color:
https://upload.wikimedia.org/wikipedia/commons/d/d9/Cotton_plantation_on_the_Mississippi%2C_1884_%28cropped%29.jpg

Photo by Timothy O'Sullivan
Source: Library of Congress

Think About It

1. What do you think the women in the photo are doing? What might the man be doing?

2. Can you guess the function of the house?

3. What type of document is shown at the right?

4. Explain why the cotton gin indirectly led to the increase in slavery even though it made the job of picking out the seeds less tedious.

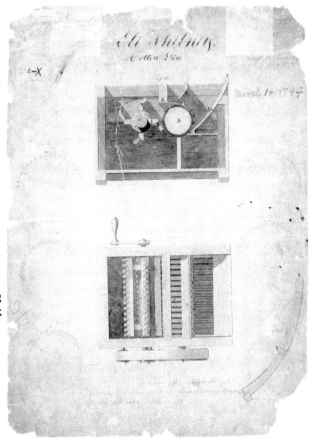

Source: Library of Congress
Office of Patents and Trademarks

Tariffs

Background Information

Tariffs are taxes imposed by a government on goods and services imported from other countries. The North and South felt very differently about them. The Northern states favored tariffs because they made foreign goods more expensive and, therefore, less competitive. The Southern states, on the other hand, were against tariffs. They did not have very much manufacturing and wanted to be able to get the imported goods at a lower price.

In 1846 the Polk administration enacted what became known as the Walker Tariff. The Walker Tariff made moderate reductions in many tariff rates. Its intent was to increase trade between the United States and Great Britain.

"Funeral Obsequies of Free-Trade"

The lithograph on the next page is entitled "Funeral Obsequies of Free-Trade" In it members of a funeral procession, comprising members of the administration, carry the coffin of "Free Trade."

The monument marking the grave contains the names of sixteen states.

Over the grave is a banner reading, "Here lies Free Trade! Be it understood / He would have liv'd much longer if he could."

The pall-bearers from left to right:
- George M. Dallas, Vice President of the United States;
- James K. Polk, President of the United States;
- James Buchanan, Secretary of State; and
- William L. Marcy, Secretary of War.

Transcription of what the pall-bearers are saying:

Polk: "This is a dead weight and [verry] heavy Mr. Vice."

Dallas: "I agree with every thing you say Mr. President. If you were to insist that the moon was made of green Cheese I would swear to it for a Consideration."

Buchanan: "I say, army lower down your side a little, you are throwing all the weight on me."

Marcy: "Raise your side, state and then we'll throw the whole weight on our leaders."

The mourners are various supporters: editor Thomas Ritchie (called "Mother Ritchie" and dressed as a woman); senators John C. Calhoun and George McDuffie; and congressmen Ambrose H. Sevier, Robert Barnwell Rhett, and Dixon Hall Lewis.

Transcription of what the mourners are saying:

Ritchie: "If he should be resuscitated! What a paragraph it would make in my paper!! Nous Verrons."

Senator Calhoun: "Hung be the heavens with black!"

Senator McDuffie: "If the whigs should get in we must resort to Nullification!"

Sevier: "This sticks in my gizzard!"

Lewis: "We must grin and bear it, though it makes me feel very heavy!"

Rhett: "A [plagu] of this sighing! it wells one up most villainously!"

Source: Library of Congress

Think About It

1. What is meant by "Funeral Obsequies"?

2. What is in the coffin?

3. What do the states listed on the grave marker have in common?

4. Two names on the grave marker are larger than the others. Why?

5. Alabama, Arkansas, Illinois, Indiana, Louisiana, Michigan, Mississippi, Missouri, South Carolina, Tennessee, and Virginia are missing from the grave marker. Why, do you suppose, did the artist omit them?

6. Secretary of State Buchanan received criticism for his support of the Walker Tariff. Explain.

7. In the lower margin is this statement: "This unfortunate youth died of Home Consumption & was buried at Washington in Nov: 1846." Explain.

"Slave Auction at Richmond, Virginia"

Background Information

With the growth of plantations and their reliance on slaves also came the growth of a new industry—the slave auction. The largest slave auction ever was held on March 2, 1859, by Pierce M. Butler. At that auction 436 men, women, children, and infants were sold to the highest bidders. All 436 had been born on Butler's plantation.

The pen-and-ink sketch below is entitled "Slave Auction at Richmond, Virginia." It accompanied an article by the same name that was published in the *Illustrated London News* on September 27, 1856. Both were created by Eyre Crowe. He began his description of the slave auction in his essay in this way: "As no pen, we think, can adequately delineate the choking sense of horror which overcomes one on first witnessing these degrading spectacles, we prefer limiting ourselves to mere description of what we saw."

Think About It

1. Evaluate the fact that the occasion was referred to as "The Weeping Time."

2. Do you think Crowe was sympathetic to the auctioneer or to the slaves? Explain.

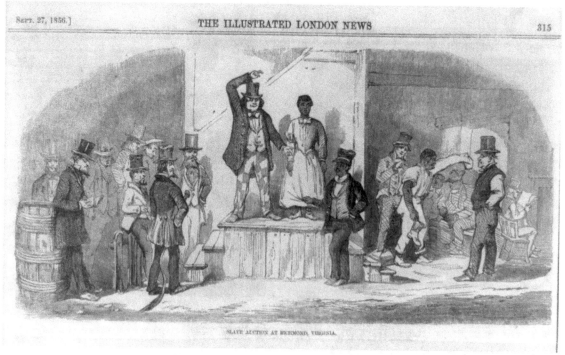

"Slave Auction at Richmond, Virginia," 1856.
Source: Library of Congress.

The Election of 1860

Background Information

By the 1860 presidential election, the North and South had become deeply divided over the issue of slavery. Candidates for four political parties emerged: Abraham Lincoln for the Republican Party; Stephen Douglas for the Democratic Party; John Breckinridge for the Southern Democrats, who had broken away from the Democratic Party; and John Bell for the Constitutional Union Party, which comprised displeased Democrats, former Whigs, and others.

The election was held on November 6, 1860. Lincoln did not win any of the slave states, but he did win all the Northern states except New Jersey, which he split with Douglas. Abraham Lincoln won the election and became the sixteenth president of the United States. His vice-president was Hannibal Hamlin.

Photograph by Alexander Hessler
Source: Library of Congress

Although some Republicans wanted to abolish slavery, the party took a more moderate position and attempted only to prevent its expansion. Lincoln's main goal was to preserve the Union, but he had expressed a dislike for the practice of slavery and had proposed antislavery legislation as a member of the U.S. House of Representatives. Many Southerners, therefore, feared his election would lead to abolition.

Photographer Unknown (Possibly Alexander Gardner)
Source: Library of Congress

Think About It

1. It is believed that this was the first time an event of this type was photographed. Can you guess what is happening? (Lincoln is under the wooden construction erected in front of the building.)

2. What building is this? Why was there construction?

"The Political Quadrille, Music by Dred Scott"

This political cartoon first appeared in *Harper's Weekly* in 1860. It was described as "a general parody on the 1860 presidential contest, highlighting the impact of the Dred Scott decision on the race."

Think About It

1. What is meant by a "quadrille"? If you are not familiar with the word, does the political cartoon give you a clue?

2. In your opinion, why did the artist place Dred Scott in the center playing the fiddle?

3. Explain the significance of how each of the four candidates was depicted in the cartoon.

4. Do you notice anything unusual about the way any of the dancers is depicted?

Library of Congress:
Originally Printed in *Harper's Weekly*, "The Political Quadrille: Music by Dred Scott"

© **Barbara M. Peller**

Secession of 1860 and Fort Sumter

Background Information

Secession from the Union had been threatened from time to time, but it didn't become a reality until December 20, 1860. On that date South Carolina seceded. In the following months ten other Southern states did the same.

Although the 1860 Republican platform did not include the desire to eliminate slavery in states where it was legal, many Southerners believed that the ultimate goal of the new Republican Party was the eventual abolition of slavery in all parts of the United States. These beliefs were especially strong in South Carolina.

When Abraham Lincoln was elected as the first Republican President, South Carolina was ready, and on December 20, 1860, the state seceded from the Union. It explained the reasons for this decision in its "Declaration of the Causes of Secession." By January 1861, six other slave states had seceded: Mississippi, Florida, Alabama, Georgia, Louisiana, and Texas. The seven states set up a provisional government in Montgomery, Alabama, and named the new government the Confederate States of America, often simply referred to as the Confederacy.

Fort Sumter

When the Confederacy met in Montgomery, Alabama, in February 1861, the delegates agreed that all forts located in states that were part of the Confederate States of America should be under Confederate control. They concluded that those forts should be acquired by negotiation, if possible, and by force, if not.

Among those forts was Fort Sumter, which was located in Charleston Harbor in South Carolina. The Confederates tried to convince the Union to give up its stronghold on the fort, but the Union was determined to hold onto it. Negotiation failed. The Confederates, therefore, decided that force was necessary. Early in the morning on April 12, 1861, they bombarded Fort Sumter.

The siege lasted thirty-three hours. At 2:30 in the afternoon on April 13, the Union commander surrendered. The next day, he and his men evacuated the fort.

The American Civil War Begins!

Following the incident at Fort Sumter, four more Southern slave states—Virginia, North Carolina, Arkansas, and Tennessee—seceded, bringing the total to eleven. The four border states—Missouri, Kentucky, Maryland, and Delaware—did not. (The western part of Virginia broke away from the state and eventually formed a new state, West Virginia. West Virginia remained in the Union.)

In May 1861—after Virginia seceded—the Confederate capital was moved from Montgomery, Alabama, to Richmond, Virginia,

The document below was sent on April 18, 1861, following the Union withdrawal from Fort Sumter. A transcription is on the following page.

S.S. BALTIC.OFF SANDY HOOK APR.EIGHTEENTH.TEN THIRTY A.M. .VIA

NEW YORK. . HON.S.CAMERON. SECY.WAR. WASHN. HAVING DEFENDED

FORT SUMTER FOR THIRTY FOUR HOURS UNTIL THE QUARTERS WERE EN

TIRELY BURNED THE MAIN GATES DESTROYED BY FIRE.THE GORGE WALLS

SERIOUSLY INJURED.THE MAGAZINE SURROUNDED BY FLAMES AND ITS

DOOR CLOSED FROM THE EFFECTS OF HEAT .FOUR BARRELLS AND THREE

CARTRIDGES OF POWDER ONLY BEING AVAILABLE AND NO PROVISIONS

REMAINING BUT PORK.I ACCEPTED TERMS OF EVACUATION OFFERED BY

GENERAL BEAUREGARD BEING ON SAME OFFERED BY HIM ON THE ELEV

ENTH INST.PRIOR TO THE COMMENCEMENT OF HOSTILITIES AND MARCHED

OUT OF THE FORT SUNDAY AFTERNOON THE FOURTEENTH INST.WITH

COLORS FLYING AND DRUMS BEATING.BRINGING AWAY COMPANY AND

PRIVATE PROPERTY AND SALUTING MY FLAG WITH FIFTY GUNS. ROBERT

ANDERSON.MAJOR FIRST ARTILLERY.COMMANDING.

Source: National Archives

Transcription

S. S. BALTIC. OFF SANDY HOOK APR. EIGHTEENTH. TEN THIRTY A.M. .VIA NEW YORK. . HON. S. CAMERON. SECY. WAR. WASHN. HAVING DEFENDED FORT SUMTER FOR THIRTY FOUR HOURS UNTIL THE QUARTERS WERE EN TIRELY BURNED THE MAIN GATES DESTROYED BY FIRE. THE GORGE WALLS SERIOUSLY INJURED. THE MAGAZINE SURROUNDED BY FLAMES AND ITS DOOR CLOSED FROM THE EFFECTS OF HEAT .FOUR BARRELLS AND THREE CARTRIDGES OF POWDER ONLY BEING AVAILABLE AND NO PROVISIONS REMAINING BUT PORK. I ACCEPTED TERMS OF EVACUATION OFFERED BY GENERAL BEAUREGARD BEING ON SAME OFFERED BY HIM ON THE ELEV ENTH INST. PRIOR TO THE COMMENCEMENT OF HOSTILITIES AND MARCHED OUT OF THE FORT SUNDAY AFTERNOON THE FOURTEENTH INST. WITH COLORS FLYING AND DRUMS BEATING. BRINGING AWAY COMPANY AND PRIVATE PROPERTY AND SALUTING MY FLAG WITH FIFTY GUNS. ROBERT ANDERSON. MAJOR FIRST ARTILLERY, COMMANDING.

Think About It

1. What type of document is this? Who sent it? What was its purpose?

2. To whom was the document sent and what position did that person hold?

3. What were the reasons for the evacuation?

4. What does the document tell us about the terms of the evacuation?

5. Where was the document created?

"The Union Is Dissolved!"

Printing of the broadside shown below began on December 20, 1861. It is believed to be the first Confederate imprint.

Think About It

1. What is the name of the newspaper that published this broadside?

2. According to the document, what was repealed and what was the result?

3. What purpose do you think broadsides like this served?

CHARLESTON

MERCURY

EXTRA:

Passed unanimously at 1.15 o'clock, P.M., December 20th, 1860.

AN ORDINANCE

To dissolve the Union between the State of South Carolina and other States united with her under the compact entitled "The Constitution of the United States of America."

We, the People of the State of South Carolina, in Convention assembled, do declare and ordain, and it is hereby declared and ordained,

That the Ordinance adopted by us in Convention, on the twenty-third day of May, in the year of our Lord one thousand seven hundred and eighty-eight, whereby the Constitution of the Untied States of America was ratified, and also, all Acts and parts of Acts of the General Assembly of this State, ratifying amendments of the said Constitution, are hereby repealed; and that the union now subsisting between South Carolina and other States, under the name of "The United States of America," is hereby dissolved.

THE

UNION

IS

DISSOLVED!

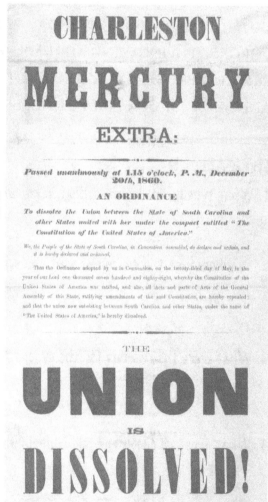

Jefferson Davis

Background Information

Jefferson Davis had represented Mississippi in both the Senate and the House of Representatives. He had also served as Secretary of War under President Pierce; nevertheless, when Mississippi seceded, he switched loyalties.

The Confederate Convention in Montgomery, Alabama, chose Jefferson Davis as provisional, or temporary, president in February 1861. On November 6, 1861, he was officially elected to a six-year term. He was inaugurated as the first and only President of the Confederacy on February 22, 1862.

The photo of Davis was taken by Matthew Brady. Brady is known for his photography of the American Civil War and is often called the Father of Photojournalism. For other photographs by Matthew Brady, visit the National Archives Website:
https://www.archives.gov/education/lessons/brady-photos

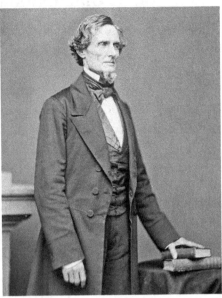

Photograph by Matthew Brady
Source: National Archives

"Jeff Davis Reaping the Harvest"

This print was created for the October 26, 1861, issue of *Harper's Weekly*.

Think About It

1. What is Jefferson Davis doing in the print?

2. Describe the mood that is created by this print. What elements help create that mood?

3. In your opinion, which side did the creator of the print blame for the loss of life caused by the Civil War?

The First Battle of Bull Run (Manassas)

Background Information

The First Battle of Bull Run, called the First Battle of Manassas by the Confederates, began on July 21, 1861. President Lincoln ordered Brigadier General Irvin McDowell and his 35,000 troops stationed in Washington, DC, to march south. He wanted them to attack the approximately 20,000 Confederate troops under General P.G.T. Beauregard. Lincoln thought he could put an early end to the war if he could open the way to Richmond. He knew that most of the men in McDowell's troops had signed up for only 90 days and that they were ill prepared; however, the Confederates also lacked training, so they went ahead with the plan.

Things did not go well for the Union. As feared, many left when their 90 days were up. Also, McDowell's forces took longer than anticipated to reach the Confederates, who were camped near Manassas Junction along a stream called Bull Run. The delay allowed Beauregard's reinforcements to get there.

About 18,000 men on each side actually took part in the fighting. Although not as bloody as future battles of the war would be, the number of men killed and wounded was much greater than either side had expected. In the end, the Confederates were victorious, but they were too inexperienced and too unorganized to take real advantage of their victory.

The Union retreat began in an orderly fashion; however, the road back to Washington, DC, was filled with carriages carrying congressmen, their families, and other onlookers. They had come to witness what they thought would be a quick Union victory. The result was complete chaos.

"The First Battle of Bull Run, VA. Sunday Afternoon July 21, 1861"

Transcription of what is written on the bottom:

THE FIRST BATTLE OF BULL RUN, VA. SUNDAY AFTERNOON JULY 21, 1861

RETREAT OF THE FEDERAL ARMY UNDER GEN McDOWELL UPON CENTREVILLE— THE RESERVE DIVISION OF COL. MILES COVERING THE RETREAT AND REPELLING THE CONFEDERATE CAVALRY.

PANIC AMONG THE TEAMSTERS AND CIVILIANS, AND GENERAL STAMPEDE TOWARDS ARLINGTON HEIGHTS

Source: Library of Congress

Think About It

1. What event is depicted in the above illustration?

2. Describe the scene depicted in the above illustration.

3. What appears to be the main cause of the chaos?

4. Which side is retreating? How do you know (in addition to the writing below the image)?

5. Why, do you think, did the artist include "Sunday Afternoon" in the title?

Spying on the Enemy

Background Information

Both sides utilized spies during the war. One of the best known spies of the era was a widow named Rose O'Neal Greenhow. The social contacts she had made because of her late husband's position with the State Department proved invaluable. She and the ladies she recruited were effective in assisting the Confederates during the early years of the war. They are credited (or blamed, depending upon your point of view) with supplying General Beauregard with vital information about Union reinforcements during the First Battle of Bull Run. It is said that dressed as a simple farm girl, one of the ladies carried the information in a coded letter, which she kept hidden in her hair.

Greenhow received this note: "Our President and our General direct me to thank you. We rely upon you for further information. The Confederacy owes you a debt, ma'am." It was signed, "JORDAN. Adjutant General." The note was written on July 22, 1861.

INCIDENTS OF THE WAR.
No. 610.
MRS. GREENHOW AND DAUGHTER,
Imprisoned in the Old Capitol, Washington.

Photograph by Matthew Brady
Source: National Archives

Greenhow was eventually captured by Allan Pinkerton, who founded the Pinkerton National Detective Agency. She was first imprisoned in her home, but later she and her young daughter were moved to the Old Capitol Prison. "Rebel Rose," as she was known, continued her espionage activities from prison. The above photograph was taken while in the Old Capitol Prison.

Think About It

1. To whom did the words "our President" in the note refer?

2. To what debt did the note refer? How do you know?

3. This coded letter, written on mourning paper, was used by "Rebel Rose." Can you guess how experts know it was mourning paper? Why might she have used it? What would have been needed to decode the letter?

Ironclads
The Battle of the *Monitor* and the *Merrimac*

Background Information

The use of ironclad ships was among the many military advancements achieved during the American Civil War. They were created by covering wooden ships with armor of iron plates. This was a vast improvement because it prevented the ships from catching fire during attack.

The most famous battle between ironclads took place in Hampton Roads, Virginia, a harbor in the mouth of the James River. This naval battle is better known today as the Battle of the *Monitor* and the *Merrimac*. The *Merrimac* was originally built in the North, but it was in the Norfolk, Virginia, naval yard when the war began. The Confederates renamed it the *Virginia*, but the ship is usually referred to as the *Merrimac*. They cut off the upper hull and had the vessel covered in iron armor. The *Monitor,* a Union warship, was also clad in iron.

The *Merrimac, or Virginia,* was under the command of Commodore Franklin Buchanan. The *Monitor* was commanded by Lieutenant John Worden. The two ironclads met on March 9, 1862. This was one day after the *Merrimac*—with the assistance of other Confederate vessels—had fired on the Union blockade at Newport News, Virginia. The blockade had been cutting off Norfolk and Richmond from international trade.

The clash between the *Merrimac* and the *Monitor* began the next day when the *Monitor* came to the aid of the other Union vessels. Spectators from both the Union and the Confederacy began to gather. Some watched from the decks of vessels and some from the shoreline.

Neither crew was well trained, so much of the fire coming from both sides was ineffective. Although the *Monitor* was much smaller than the *Merrimac,* it was also faster and easier to maneuver. On the other hand, the larger *Merrimac* was stronger and able to hold more guns. In fact, the *Merrimac* had ten guns and the *Monitor* only two.

The battle lasted several hours. Although it was indecisive, because the *Merrimac* pulled back to Norfolk, the smaller *Monito*r is often credited with victory. However, the Confederates also had reason to use the incidents involving the ironclads to boost morale. The Confederate success the day before at Newport News gave the South reason to be optimistic that it would be able to stop the Northern blockade.

Neither ship had an impressive end of service. The crew of the *Merrimac, or Virginia,* destroyed the vessel when the Confederates left Norfolk in May of the same year. The *Monitor* sank during a storm that occurred off Cape Hatteras, North Carolina, that December.

Although each side claimed victory after the Battle of the *Monitor* and the *Merrimac,* one thing became clear. The clash of these two ironclads marked the beginning of a new era in naval warfare.

"Terrific Combat Between the 'Monitor' 2 Guns & 'Merrimac' 10 Guns"

The lithograph depicted below was published in New York by Currier & Ives about 1862.

Transcription of what is written at the bottom of the lithograph:

THE FIRST FIGHT BETWEEN IRON CLAD SHIPS OF WAR,

TERRIFIC COMBAT BETWEEN THE "MONITOR" 2 GUNS & "MERRIMAC" 10 GUNS.

IN HAMPTON ROADS, MARCH 9TH 1862.

In which the little "Monitor" whipped the "Merrimac" and the whole "School" of Rebel Steamers.

Lithograph Published by Currier & Ives in 1862
Source: Library of Congress

Note: The original is in color. To view it in color, use the following url:
https://www.loc.gov/resource/ppmsca.31277/

© **Barbara M. Peller**

Letter to S.R. Mallory: Transcription

Hon. S. R. MALLORY,
Secretary of the Navy.

Report of Major-General Huger, C.S. Army, commanding Department of Norfolk, on the impact of ironclad warships in warfare.

HEADQUARTERS DEPARTMENT OF NORFOLK,
Norfolk, Va., March 10, 1862.

SIR: I telegraphed yesterday to the Secretary of War the fact of the naval engagement on the 8th and 9th instants. As the battle was fought by the navy, Flag-Officer Forrest will no doubt report to the Navy Department the result of the engagement.

The batteries at Sewell's Point opened fire on the steamers *Minnesota* and *Roanoke,* which attempted on the 8th to pass to Newport News to the assistance of the frigates attacked by the *Virginia*. The *Minnesota* ran aground before reaching there. The *Roanoke* was struck several times, and for some cause turned around and went back to Old Point.

The two sailing vessels (*Cumberland* and *Congress*) were destroyed—the first sunk and the other burned by the *Virginia*—and on the 9th the *Minnesota;* still aground, would probably have been destroyed but for the ironclad battery of the enemy called, I think, the *Monitor.* The *Virginia* and this battery were in actual contact, without inflicting serious injury on either.

At 2 p. m. on yesterday, the 9th, all our vessels came up to the navy yard for repairs. The *Virginia*, I understand, has gone into dock for repairs, which will be made at once. This action shows the power and endurance of ironclad vessels. Cannon shot do not harm them, and they can pass batteries or destroy large ships. A vessel like the *Virginia* or the *Monitor,* with her two guns, can pass any of our batteries with impunity. The only means of stopping them is by vessels of the same kind. The *Virginia*, being the most powerful, can stop the *Monitor,* but a more powerful one would run her down or ashore. As the enemy can build such boats faster than we, they could, when so prepared, overcome any place accessible by water. How these powerful machines are to be stopped is a problem I can not solve. At present, in the *Virginia;* we have the advantage; but we can not tell how long this may last.

I remain very respectfully, your obedient servant,

BENJ. HUGER,
Major-General, Commanding.

General S. COOPER,
Adjutant and Inspector General

Think About It: Lithograph

1. Which is the *Monitor?* Which is the *Merrimac?* How do you know?

2. Do you think the creator of the lithograph was pro-Union or pro-Confederate? What makes you think that?

3. Research and report on other technological advancements that affected the military during the Civil War. Which side benefitted the most and why?

4. What do you see in the background?

Think About It: Letter

1. What does the letter describe?

2. Who wrote the letter and who were the recipients?

3. On which side were the sender and the recipients? How do you know?

4. What were the author's conclusions?

West Virginia Becomes a State

Background Information

The western part of Virginia was very different from the rest of the state in population, culture, and geography. There was also a major economic difference between the two regions. The economy in the western part of the state did not depend upon free labor; very few residents were slave owners.

The mountaineers in the western counties did not like the fact that most of the power in the state lay with those living in the eastern Coastal Plain region known as the Tidewater. They referred to those powerful men as the "tidewater aristocrats" or the "tidewater gentry." Most of the laws passed in the state favored those influential men; the needs of the western counties for roads, railroads, and other improvements were largely ignored. The idea of separation from the rest of the state was in the minds of many westerners.

It wasn't a surprise, therefore, that when delegates to the Virginia Secession Convention voted to secede from the Union, only five of the thirty-one delegates from the western part of the state voted in favor of secession. Disagreement grew. The mountaineers of the West wanted to stay in the Union, but in order to do that, they first had to secede from the state of Virginia.

On June 11, 1861, a convention was held. Its purpose was to separate from the rest of the state in order to form a new state. The delegates held that they were forming a "restored government" with its capital in Wheeling. They reasoned that because the Confederate legislature in Richmond was not legal, the state offices were vacant; therefore, they appointed new state officials. Francis Pierpoint became the new governor. The new state legislature elected two U.S. Senators and three U.S. Representatives. In order to vote, an oath to the United States Constitution was required.

The Wheeling Convention met several times between 1861 until 1863. It overwhelmingly passed an ordinance to separate from Virginia and to form a new state; however, there was some disagreement regarding the name. The delegates eventually decided to take a vote with the understanding that the majority would rule. The final result was as follows: "West Virginia" 30, "Kanawha" 9, "Western Virginia" 2, "Allegheny" 2, and "Augusta" 1. The new state would be named West Virginia.

Before West Virginia could enter the Union, it had to accept emancipation of slaves as a condition. It did this and entered the Union on July 4, 1863, as the nation's thirty-fifth state. The U.S. Senate seated the new senators.

Think About It

1. Underline the sentence in Article IV, Section 3, of the U.S. Constitution that explains why West Virginia had to secede from Virginia before it could enter the Union as a new state.

Article IV, Section 3. New states may be admitted by the Congress into this union; but no new states shall be formed or erected within the jurisdiction of any other state; nor any state be formed by the junction of two or more states, or parts of states, without the consent of the legislatures of the states concerned as well as of the Congress.

The Congress shall have power to dispose of and make all needful rules and regulations respecting the territory or other property belonging to the United States; and nothing in this Constitution shall be so construed as to prejudice any claims of the United States, or of any particular state.

2. When Section 1 of the ordinance was read, several delegates wanted a change. Read the introduction of the section and the excerpts of two delegates' (Sinsel and Brown) views shown below.

> *Section 1: The State of Kanawha shall be and remain one of the United States of America. The Constitution of the United States, and the laws and treaties made in pursuance thereof, shall be the supreme law of the land.*

Harmon Sinsel of Taylor County had this point of view:

> *"Mr. President, one reason I have for striking it out is that I am a Virginian; I was born and raised in Virginia, and I have ever been proud of the name. I admit that Virginians have done wrong—that many of them in this rebellion have disgraced themselves; but that has not weaned me from the name. When we look back to history and see the origin of the name—Virginia, from the Virgin Queen—the queen who swayed the scepter of England with so much glory and renown—we might almost go back a little further to Virginia, the Virgin. It always makes me think of the Virgin Mary, the mother of our blessed Redeemer. It is a name that I almost revere; and I am utterly opposed to leaving it out and substituting the name Kanawha in its stead."*

William G. Brown of Kanawha County had a different point of view:

> *"In changing this name it seems to me the Convention ought to inquire as to the propriety of it, and whether there is any better name to be selected. In looking at our power in this matter I understand that we are called here in pursuance of law. I understand that we are not a heterogeneous mass of individuals assembled here to follow the bent and inclinations of ourselves, but assembled here in legal form, under a prescribed law of the State - a law emanating from a convention assembled in pursuance of and with the assent of the legislature as within that law, carried into effect and ratified so far as our action here is concerned, by the free will of the people. That ordinance prescribes definitely the name of the State proposed to be erected; and it becomes a question not whether this or that or any other name shall be the name of the new State but submits the question definitely to the people within the proposed boundaries whether they will form the new State as proposed with the name prescribed. I have understood from gentlemen who were in that Convention that the name itself was a compromise. But whether it were a compromise or not I maintain the people have ratified this question and have determined by our presence here that this new State shall exist and that it shall be called Kanawha."*

Briefly explain each point of view.

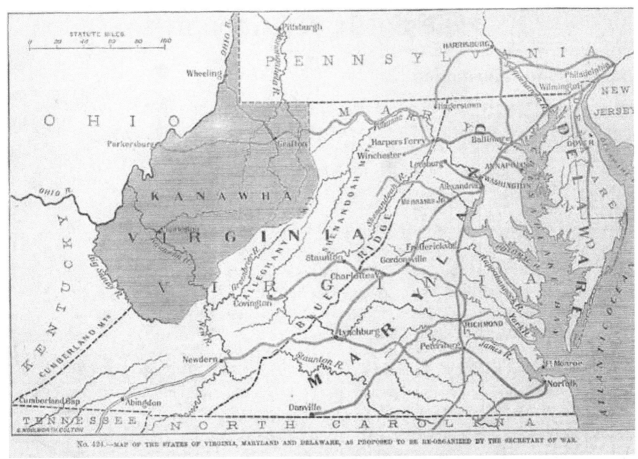

Source: Wikimedia Commons

3. Daniel Lamb of Wheeling objected to any form of the name Virginia:

"Sir, I have been an inhabitant of western Virginia for thirty odd years. During that time what have we received here but oppression, and outrage I may say, from the State of Virginia. During that time our people having been constantly complaining of the course of policy that has been forced upon them. We have been denied by the State of Virginia, for many long years, our proper share in the representation and government of the State."

He was angered by the way the eastern part of the state treated the western part of the state. Why did the eastern region have more power?

4. The 1862 map above shows the proposed state of Kanawha. It is from Frank Leslie's *Pictorial History of the American Civil War*, 1862. Study the map and use geographic features to explain why many in the western part of the state favored separation.

The Battle of Antietam

Background Information

The bloodiest one-day battle of the American Civil War took place on September 17, 1862, in Sharpsburg, Maryland, along a creek called Antietam. The battle marked the end of the Maryland Campaign, which was the first invasion of the North by the Army of Northern Virginia.

The Confederate troops were led by General Robert E. Lee, whose victory at the Second Battle of Bull Run (Manassas) encouraged him to keep up the offensive. These were among his immediate goals: to move the war to the North; to encourage Maryland, a slave-holding border state, to join the Confederacy; to gain control of Washington; and to obtain much needed supplies.

General Lee divided his troops. He ordered General "Stonewall" Jackson to take half of the troops to capture the Union forces in Harpers Ferry, West Virginia. Lee moved the remaining troops towards South Mountain, the northern extension of the Blue Ridge Mountain range in Maryland and Pennsylvania.

General Robert E. Lee
Photograph by Julian Vannerson
Source: Library of Congress

General George B. McClellan
Photograph by Matthew Brady

The Union's Army of the Potomac was led by General George B. McClellan. Although the Union loss at Manassas had demoralized the troops, McClellan regrouped, and he and his men marched towards South Mountain to confront General Lee.

The Confederates were unsuccessful in their attempt to block the Union troops, and Lee considered a retreat. When he learned that Stonewall Jackson had defeated the Union troops at Harpers Ferry, however, he changed his mind. Instead of retreating, he ordered the troops to reorganize at Antietam Creek.

What would turn out to be a 12-hour battle began on September 17. By the time it ended, about 23,000 men were either dead, missing, or wounded, making the Battle of Antietam the bloodiest one-day battle of the war. Although the battle itself was not a decisive victory for either side, Lee was forced to retreat, ending his first invasion into the North.

Lee's retreat did have an important effect. It afforded President Lincoln the opportunity he sought to issue a Preliminary Emancipation Proclamation; he did so on September 22, 1862.

© **Barbara M. Peller**

The Dead of Antietam

These photographs were taken by Alexander Gardner, who worked for Mathew Brady. When Gardner returned to New York, they were displayed as part of an exhibition called "The Dead of Antietam."

Think About It

1. How might Alexander Gardner's photographs have changed people's views of the war?

2. Describe the mood evoked by these photos. How do you think these and similar photos made people feel?

3. Look at the top photo. What did people learn about the way the fallen soldiers were buried?

Letters from Antietam

Primary sources in the form of letters to friends and loved ones and diary entries provide historians with a wealth of information about what the soldiers were thinking and feeling. Two examples follow.

Sunday Sept. 21, 1862

Dear Folks,

On the 8th we struck up the refrain of "Maryland, My Maryland!" and camped in an apple orchard. We went hungry, for six days not a morsel of bread or meat had gone in our stomachs—and our menu consisted of apple; and corn. We toasted, we burned, we stewed, we boiled, we roasted these two together, and singly, until there was not a man whose form had not caved in, and who had not a bad attack of diarrhea. Our under-clothes were foul and hanging in strips, our socks worn out, and half of the men were bare-footed, many were lame and were sent to the rear; others, of sterner stuff, hobbled along and managed to keep up, while gangs from every company went off in the surrounding country looking for food. . . Many became ill from exposure and starvation, and were left on the road. The ambulances were full, and the whole route was marked with a sick, lame, limping lot, that straggled to the farm-houses that lined the way, and who, in all cases, succored and cared for them. . .

In an hour after the passage of the Potomac the command continued the march through the rich fields of Maryland. The country people lined the roads, gazing in open-eyed wonder upon the long lines of infantry . . .and as far as the eye could reach, was the glitter of the swaying points of the bayonets. It was the first ragged Rebels they had ever seen, and though they did not act either as friends or foes, still they gave liberally, and every haversack was full that day at least. No houses were entered—no damage was done, and the farmers in the vicinity must have drawn a long breath as they saw how safe their property was in the very midst of the army.

Alexander Hunter

Think About It: Letter from Alexander Hunter

1. Was the writer of this letter on the Confederate or Union side? How do you know?

2. Describe their diet while camped in the apple orchard.

3. Describe the general condition of the men. What happened to the men who could not keep up?

4. How did the farmers they passed treat the soldiers? Why were the farmers relieved?

5. How would you have felt if you were Alexander Hunter's family receiving this letter?

A strong, sturdy-looking Reb was coming laboriously on with a Yank of no small proportions perched on his shoulders. Wonderingly I joined the group surrounding and accompanying them at every step, and then I learned why all this especial demonstration; why the Union soldiers cheered and again cheered this Confederate soldier, not because of the fact alone that he had brought into the hospital a sorely wounded Federal soldier, who must have died from hemorrhage had he been left on the field, but from the fact, that was palpable at a glance, that the Confederate too was wounded. He was totally blind; a Yankee bullet had passed directly across and destroyed both eyes, and the light for him had gone out forever. But on he marched, with his brother in misery perched on his sturdy shoulders. He would accept no assistance until his partner announced to him that they had reached their goal - the field hospital. It appears that they lay close together on the field, and after the roar of battle had been succeeded by that painfully intense silence that hangs over a hard-contested battlefield; where the issue is yet in doubt, and where a single rifle shot on the skirmish line falls on your ear like the crack of a thousand cannon. The groans of the wounded Yank reached the alert ears of his sightless Confederate neighbor, who called to him, asking him the nature and extent of his wounds. On learning the serious nature of them, he said: "Now, Yank, I can't see, or I'd get out of here mighty lively. Some darned Yank has shot away my eyes, but I feel as strong otherwise as ever. If you think you can get on my back and do the seeing, I will do the walking, and we'll sail into some hospital where we can both receive surgical treatment." This programme had been followed and with complete success.

We assisted the Yank to alight from his Rebel war-horse, and you can rest assured that loud and imperative call was made for the surgeons to give not only the Yank, but his noble Confederate partner, immediate and careful attention.

J. O. Smith

(Roulette Farm Field Hospital)

Think About It: Letter from J.O. Smith

6. What prompted J.O. Smith to write this letter?

7. How did the Yank and the Reb cooperate with one another?

8. The home of William and Margaret Roulette was used after the battle as a field hospital for Union soldiers. Why did the people in the field hospital cry for help as strongly for the Reb as for the Yank as they entered the hospital?

© Barbara M. Peller

Using Primary Sources to Teach U.S. History: The American Civil War 49

Clara Barton

Background Information

Clarissa Harlowe Barton was born in Massachusetts in 1821. Although today she is honored for her work helping the wounded during the Civil War, she had no formal training as a nurse. Clara, as she was called, worked first as a teacher. Then—from 1853 to 1857—she had a job as a clerk in the Patent Office in Washington, DC; however, her outspoken antislavery opinions led to her dismissal from that job.

Photograph by Matthew Brady
Source: National Park Service

When war broke out in 1861, Clara volunteered to help care for wounded soldiers at first in the city hospitals and then in the battlefields. In July 1861 she assisted wounded soldiers at the First Battle of Bull Run (First Manassas). Just as important, she set up a network to get and distribute much needed supplies.

Clara Barton asked President Lincoln for permission to transport supplies to the various battlefields. She received that permission on August 3, 1862. It's no wonder that the men often called her the "Angel of the Battlefield."

Time and time again she put her own life in danger to help others. This was never more apparent than at the Battle of Antietam, Maryland. The surgeons there were in dire need of medical supplies. She helped them obtain those supplies, but was so exhausted and run-down following the battle that she developed typhoid fever. Even so, that did not prevent her from travelling with the Army of the Potomac in pursuit of the Confederates as they retreated into Virginia.

In March 1865 President Lincoln authorized Clara Barton to deal with the problem of finding the large number of missing soldiers. She established the Office of Correspondence with Friends of the Missing Men of the United States Army. Under her direction, the bureau carried out an intensive search. She was greatly aided by Dorence Atwater. While a prisoner of war in Andersonville Prison, Atwater was assigned the task of keeping a record of the dead; while doing so, he had secretly kept a list for himself. When the Office of Correspondence closed in 1868, they had identified more than 22,000 missing men. About 13,000 of them were found in unmarked graves in Andersonville. Clara saw to it that the graves were identified and marked accordingly. In carrying out this mission, she had spent a lot of her own money. On March 10, 1866, Congress approved $15,000 to reimburse her for her expenses.

In 1869 Clara Barton travelled to Switzerland. While there, she learned about the International Red Cross. She was so impressed by the work of that organization that in 1880 she founded the American Red Cross. She was the organization's first president and remained in that office until 1904.

Clara Barton died at ninety-one years of age in 1912.

Letter to the President

To his Excellency Abraham Lincoln
President of the United States
Sir,

    I most respectfully solicit your authority and endorsement to allow me to act temporarily as general correspondent at Annapolis Maryland, having in view the reception and answering of letters from the friends of our prisoners now being exchanged.

    It will be my object also to obtain and furnish all possible information in regard to those that have died during their confinement.

    Hoping that the objects contemplated may commend themselves to your favorable consideration.

    I am Most Respectfully,
    Clara Barton

Source: Library of Congress

Think About It

1. What was the purpose of this letter?

2. Describe Miss Barton's handwriting. Why, do you think, did she write in this style?

3. Clara Barton said the following in reference to her experience in Antietam. Rewrite the quotation in your own words.

    "A ball had passed between my body and the right arm which supported him, cutting through the sleeve and passing through his chest from shoulder to shoulder. There was no more to be done for him and I left him to his rest. I have never mended that hole in my sleeve."

The Emancipation Proclamation

Background Information

President Abraham Lincoln issued the Emancipation Proclamation on January 1, 1863. The following are excerpts from that document.

Excerpts from the Emancipation Proclamation (1863)

Whereas, on the twenty-second day of September, in the year of our Lord one thousand eight hundred and sixty-two, a proclamation was issued by the President of the United States, containing, among other things, the following, to wit:

"That on the first day of January, in the year of our Lord one thousand eight hundred and sixty-three, all persons held as slaves within any State or designated part of a State, the people whereof shall then be in rebellion against the United States, shall be then, thenceforward, and forever free; and the Executive Government of the United States, including the military and naval authority thereof, will recognize and maintain the freedom of such persons, and will do no act or acts to repress such persons, or any of them, in any efforts they may make for their actual freedom.

"That the Executive will, on the first day of January aforesaid, by proclamation, designate the States and parts of States, if any, in which the people thereof, respectively, shall then be in rebellion against the United States; and the fact that any State, or the people thereof, shall on that day be, in good faith, represented in the Congress of the United States by members chosen thereto at elections wherein a majority of the qualified voters of such State shall have participated, shall, in the absence of strong countervailing testimony, be deemed conclusive evidence that such State, and the people thereof, are not then in rebellion against the United States."

…

And I hereby enjoin upon the people so declared to be free to abstain from all violence, unless in necessary self-defence; and I recommend to them that, in all cases when allowed, they labor faithfully for reasonable wages.

And I further declare and make known, that such persons of suitable condition, will be received into the armed service of the United States to garrison forts, positions, stations, and other places, and to man vessels of all sorts in said service.

…

And I hereby enjoin upon the people so declared to be free to abstain from all violence, unless in necessary self-defence; and I recommend to them that, in all cases when allowed, they labor faithfully for reasonable wages.

And I further declare and make known, that such persons of suitable condition, will be received into the armed service of the United States to garrison forts, positions, stations, and other places, and to man vessels of all sorts in said service.

…

By the President: ABRAHAM LINCOLN
WILLIAM H. SEWARD, Secretary of State.

Preliminary Emancipation Proclamation

On September 22, 1862—after the Battle of Antietam—President Lincoln issued the Preliminary Emancipation Proclamation. The following is the opening paragraph of that document:

> *I, Abraham Lincoln, President of the United States of America, and Commander-in-Chief of the Army and Navy thereof, do hereby proclaim and declare that hereafter, as heretofore, the war will be prosecuted for the object of practically restoring the constitutional relation between the United States, and each of the States, and the people thereof, in which States that relation is, or may be, suspended or disturbed.*

Think About It

1. Read the opening paragraph of the Preliminary Emancipation Proclamation (shown above). What did President Lincoln cite as the reason for the war?

2. What new objective of the war was described in the Emancipation Proclamation?

3. What will happen on January 1, 1863?

4. How will the President determine which states are not in rebellion against the United States?

5. What did the President ask of the newly freed slaves?

6. What did the document say about the newly freed slaves and the military?

"Emancipation" by Thomas Nast

"Emancipation"

Thomas Nast created an illustration entitled "Emancipation" for the January 24, 1863, edition of *Harper's Weekly*. At the bottom is the following caption: "Emancipation of the Negroes, January 1863—The Past and The Future—Drawn by Mr. Thomas Nast." The illustration celebrated what Nast saw as the changes that would come about because of the Emancipation Proclamation. The complex work contains many scenes, some depicting the evils of slavery and some predicting the promise of what was to come.

In 1865 Nast created a new version of the illustration. The 1865 version contained a change in the circle at the bottom. In the original version, the image in the circle showed Father Time as an angel holding the New Year baby. The viewer could infer that the baby was about to remove the slave's shackles. In the newer edition, Nast replaced this image with a portrait of President Lincoln.

Think About It

1. What, do you think, prompted Nast to change the image in the bottom circle?

2. Above the large center circle is an illustration of Thomas Crawford's statue entitled "Freedom." How would you describe the scene inside the large center circle? What is the mood created by that scene?

3. Nast contrasted the lives of the slaves under the Confederacy with what would hopefully be their future lives as free men and women. Cite examples of the evils of slavery shown on the left half of the illustration.

4. Cite examples of what Nast predicted would be their lives as free men and women shown on the right.

5. Contrast the image over the scenes on the left with the image over the scenes on the right.

6. Contrast the images on either side of the small circle.

© **Barbara M. Peller**

HARPER'S WEEKLY
EMANCIPATION
CASHIER
PUBLIC SCHOOL
THE EMANCIPATION OF THE NEGROES, JANUARY, 1863—THE PAST AND THE FUTURE.—Drawn by Mr. Thomas Nast.—[See preceding Page.]

Source: Library of Congress

Recruitment Posters

Background Information

During the Civil War, recruitment posters were an important means of enticing men to join the service. They contained patriotic imagery, promises of bonuses, payment information, and more. Some contained symbols that would appeal to specific populations. For example, posters meant to encourage Irish recruits to enlist often had harps or shamrocks.

Think About It: "To Arms! To Arms"

1. Is this a Union or a Confederate recruitment poster? Who is doing the recruiting? According to this poster, why should men enlist with this volunteer company instead of waiting to get drafted?

2. How many recruits are needed?

3. The poster says that the recruit will receive a bounty of 50 dollars. Explain what that means.

4. What other money will the recruit receive upon being enrolled? Do we know what the monthly pay will be?

5. What must happen before a recruit can be officially enrolled?

6. Where should a man go if he is interested in joining the company?

7. What do you think the recruiters thought was the best enticement? What makes you think that?

TO ARMS! TO ARMS!

$50 BOUNTY.

Do not wait to be Drafted, but Volunteer!!

The subscribers wish to get sixty Recruits for

CAPT. STIGLEMAN'S COMPANY VIRGINIA VOLUNTEERS.

Persons wishing to enlist will find it greatly to their advantage to join this Company, as we can offer superior inducements.

You will receive pay and subsistence from the time your names are enrolled; your bounty of 50 dollars, and 25 dollars for clothing, as soon as you can be examined by an Army Surgeon.

For further particulars apply to us at Floyd Court House, Va.

LIUT. G. M. HELMS, } Recruiting
Sergt. J. W. SHELTON. } Officers.

February 22, 1862.

WE WILL ATTEND THE

PUBLIC MEETINGS

to be held at the following places
Indian Valley, Saturday, March 1st; Jackson Harriss' Stillhouse, Monday, 3rd; Jacob S. Harman's Store, Friday, 7th; Oil Mills Saturday, 8th; Copper Hill, Friday, 14th; Locust Grove, Saturday, 15th, and at Floyd Court House, March, 20th (Court day.)

Think About It: "Cavalry to the Field!"

1. According to the "Cavalry to the Field!" poster, what was the range of pay if a recruit joined the 1st Battalion N.Y. Mounted Rifles?

2. Why was the 1st Battalion N.Y. Mounted Rifles seeking recruits? How many were wanted?

3. What adjective did the Secretary of War use to describe the battalion?

4. What could each recruit expect to receive after he enlisted? Upon reaching the regiment? Upon being mustered in?

5. Use context clues to define the verb "muster." Look up the definition if you are not sure.

6. Were any patriotic symbols used?

7. Do you think this recruitment poster was an effective enticement? Explain your point of view.

Black Soldiers in the Civil War

Background Information

By the end of the Civil War, about 179,000 black men had served as soldiers in the U.S. Army; this was approximately 10% of the Union Army. Another 19,000 served in the U.S. Navy.

On March 21, 1863, Frederick Douglas, a prominent black leader in the abolitionist movement, gave a speech in Rochester, New York. In that speech he urged black men to join the Union forces.

In June 1863 recruitment of black soldiers was officially authorized by the Union Army. This prompted a group of local abolitionist leaders to meet in Philadelphia. Frederick Douglas joined them and was among the 54 men who signed the broadside. A transcription is on the next page.

Think About It

1. What was the main purpose of this poster?

2. The broadside says that race relations had changed. What was the reason for that change?

Source: Library of Congress

3. Cite some reasons given why blacks should enlist.

4. Which two incidents of valor shown by men of color did the recruitment poster cite? Research these incidents and summarize their significance.

5. Of all the reasons given, which do you think was most convincing? Can you think of any other reasons that might have been included?

Transcription of Broadside

MEN OF COLOR
TO ARMS! TO ARMS!
NOW OR NEVER

This is our golden moment! The Government of the United States calls for every Able-bodied Colored Man to enter the Army for the

Three Years' Service!

And join in Fighting the Battles of Liberty and the Union. A new era is open to us. For generations we have suffered under the horrors of slavery, outrage and wrong; our manhood has been denied, our citizenship blotted out, our souls seared and burned, our spirits cowed and crushed, and the hopes of the future of our race involved in doubt and darkness. But now our relations to the white race are changed. Now, therefore, is our most precious moment. Let us rush to arms!

FAIL NOW, & OUR RACE IS DOOMED

On this the soil of our birth. We must now awake, arise, or be forever fallen. If we value liberty, if we wish to be free in this land, if we love our country, if we love our families, our children, our home, we must strike *now* while the country calls; we must rise up in the dignity of our manhood, and show by our own right arms that we are worthy to be freemen. Our enemies have made the country believe that we are craven cowards, without soul, without manhood, without the spirit of soldiers. Shall we die with this stigma resting upon our graves? Shall we leave this inheritance of Shame to our Children? No! a thousand times NO! We WILL Rise! The alternative is upon is. Let us rather die freemen than live to be slaves. What is life without liberty? We say that we have manhood; now is the time to prove it. A nation or a people that cannot fight may be pitied, but cannot be respected. If we would be regarded *men*, if we would forever silence the tongue of Calumny, of Prejudice and Hate, let us Rise Now and Fly to Arms! We have seen what Valor and Heroism our Brothers displayed at Port Hudson and Milliken's Bend, though they are just from the galling, poisoning grasp of Slavery, they have startled the World by the most exalted heroism. If they have proved themselves heroes, cannot WE PROVE OURSELVES MEN?

ARE FREEMEN LESS BRAVE THAN SLAVES

More than a Million White Men Have Left Comfortable Homes and joined the Armies of the Union to save their Country. Cannot we leave ours, and swell the Hosts of the Union, to save our liberties, vindicate our manhood, and deserve well of our Country. MEN OF COLOR! the Englishman, the Irishman, the Frenchman, the German, the American, have been called to assert their claim to freedom and a manly character, by appeal to the sword. The day that has seen an enslaved race in arms has, in all history, seen their last trial. We now see that our last opportunity has come. If we are not lower in the scale of humanity than Englishmen, Irishmen, White Americans, and other Races, we can show it now. Men of Color, Brothers and Fathers! We appeal to you! By all your concern for yourselves and your liberties, by all your regard for God and humanity, by all your desire for Citizenship and Equality before the law, by all your love for the Country, to stop at no subterfuge, listen to nothing that shall deter you from rallying for the Army. Come Forward, and at once Enroll your Names for the Three Years' Service.

Strike now, and you are henceforth and forever Freemen!

E.D. Bassett, Wm. Whipper, D.D. Turner, Jas. McCrumell, A.S. Cassey, A.M. Green, J.W. Page, L.R. Seymour, Rev. J. Underdue, John W. Price, Augustus Dorsey, William D. Forten, Rev. Stephen Smith, N.W. Depee, Dr. J. H. Wilson, J.W. Cassey, Frederick Douglas, P.J. Armstrong, J.W. Simpson, Rev. J. B. Trusty, S. Morgan Smith, William E. Gipson, Rev. J. Boulden, Rev. J. Asher, Rev. J.C. Gibbs, Daniel George, Robert M. Adger, Heary M. Cropper, Rev. J.B. Reeve, Rev. J.A. Williams, Rev. A.L. Stanford, Thomas J. Bowers, Elijah J. Davis, John P. Burr, Robert Jones, O. V. Catto, Thos. J. Dorsey, I.D. Cliff, Jacob C. White, Morris Hall, James Needham, Rev. Elisha Weaver, Ebenezer Black, Rev. William T. Catto, James R. Gordon, Samuel Stewart, David B. Bowser, Henry Minton, Daniel Colley, J.C. White, Jr., Rev. J.P. Campbell, Rev. W.J. Alston, J.P. Johnson, Franklin Turner, Jesse E. Glasgow

U.S. Steam-Power Book and Job Printing Establishment Ledger Buildings, Third and Chestnut Streets, Philadelphia.

The Siege of Vicksburg

Background Information

The location of Vicksburg, Mississippi, high on a bluff on a bank of the Mississippi River made the city strategically important to both the Union and the Confederacy. Control of the city meant control of the great river.

Early Union efforts to gain control of Vicksburg were mostly ineffective. In the spring of 1863 Major General Ulysses S. Grant planned a siege of the city. The Vicksburg Campaign would involve about 70,000 Union troops, led by Grant, and about 29,000 Confederate troops, led by Lt. General John Pemberton.

Many, including President Lincoln, were skeptical about Grant's strategy. However, Lincoln did not interfere, and Grant stuck to his plan. Before advancing to Vicksburg, Grant turned west and captured Jackson, the capital of Mississippi. This gave the Union control of the railways leading to Vicksburg.

"Commanding General Grant,"
by Ole Peter Hansen Balling, 1865
Source: Wikimedia Commons

From Jackson, Grant and his men continued on to Vicksburg. Their assaults on May 19 and May 22 were not successful; however, the 40-day siege on Lt. Pemberton's troops that began on May 25 was. The Union gained control of the railroad, preventing the Confederates from using the rails to transport reinforcements, food, and supplies. Unable to obtain the help he needed, Pemberton surrendered.

Grant's siege of Vicksburg has been hailed as one of the most brilliant campaigns of the American Civil War. Combined with the Union victory at Port Hudson a few days later, success gave the Union control of the Mississippi River, thereby splitting the Confederacy in half. Grant's ability as a military strategist greatly impressed President Lincoln. On March 10, 1864, Lincoln appointed Ulysses S. Grant General-in-Chief of the Union armies.

Executive Mansion,

Washington, July 13, 1863.

My Dear General

I do not remember that you and I ever met personally. I write this now as a grateful acknowledgement for the almost inestimable service you have done the country. I wish to say a word further. When you first reached the vicinity of Vicksburg, I thought you should do what you finally did—march the troops across the neck, run the batteries with the transports and thus go below; and I never had any faith, except a general hope that you knew better than I, that the Yazoo-Pass expedition, and the like could succeed. When you got below, and took Port Gibson, Grand Gulf and vicinity, I thought you should go down the river and join Gen. Banks; and when you turned Northward, East of the Big Black, I feared it was a mistake. I now wish to make the personal acknowledgement that you were right and I was wrong.

Yours very truly
(Signed) A. Lincoln

[Endorsed on Envelope by Lincoln:]
To Gen. Grant — July 13. 1863.

Think About It

1. Locate Vicksburg, Mississippi, on a map. Use its location to explain its strategic importance.

2. Read the July 13, 1863, letter from President Lincoln to Ulysses S. Grant. What are the main reasons for the letter?

3. What does this letter tell you about President Lincoln?

The Battle of Gettysburg

Background Information

The three-day battle at Gettysburg, Pennsylvania, was the bloodiest battle of the American Civil War. Union casualties numbered about 23,000, and the number of Confederates who were killed or wounded was about 28,000. The battle was also a turning point in the conflict.

In the summer of 1863, General Robert E. Lee decided to carry out his second invasion of the North. (The first had been the Maryland Campaign, which ended with the Battle of Antietam.) General Lee's victory at Chancellorsville, Virginia, gave him the confidence to launch a bold invasion of Pennsylvania. He hoped that the defeat of Union troops on their own soil would encourage President Lincoln to negotiate a peace. He also hoped that a Confederate victory here would convince the Europeans to come to their assistance.

General Lee's troops—the Army of Northern Virginia—numbered about 75,000. The Union troops— the Army of the Potomac—were led by General George G. Meade, who had just replaced General Joseph Hooker as commander; that force comprised about 90,000 men.

July 1, the first day of the battle, resulted in a victory for the Confederates. They forced the Union troops to retreat to Cemetery Ridge, which was just south of the city. Confederate soldiers gathered in Seminary Ridge to the west.

It was the second day of battle that was the bloodiest. The generals under Lee made the mistake of allowing the Union's reinforcements to arrive. Therefore, the Union was able to fortify their position and stop the Confederate attack.

General Lee decided to give it another try on July 3. He ordered General Pickett to lead his 15,000 men in an attack. However, this action, which became known as "Pickett's Charge," was a failure.

The next day Lee began to move his army South. Meade and his troops followed, but Meade decided not to attack. This allowed the Confederates to cross the Potomac and return to Virginia.

Think About It

1. Read the letter on the next page. In Lincoln's view, what would have happened if General Meade had pursued General Lee?

2. Lincoln later replaced Meade as Commander of the Army of the Potomac with General Ulysses S. Grant. Find an excerpt from the letter that might explain his reasoning.

3. Have you ever written a letter to express your anger and then not sent it? If so, did venting your emotions change the way you felt? If you have not done this yourself, evaluate how effective you think this would be.

An Unsent Letter

Below is the transcription of a letter President Abraham Lincoln wrote to General George G. Meade on July 14, 1863. Lincoln did not send the letter. It was found among his papers after his death.

Executive Mansion,
Washington, July 14, 1863.
Major General Meade

I have just seen your despatch to Gen. Halleck, asking to be relieved of your command, because of a supposed censure of mine—I am very—very—grateful to you for the magnificent success you gave the cause of the country at Gettysburg; and I am sorry now to be the author of the slightest pain to you— But I was in such deep distress myself that I could not restrain some expression of it— I had been oppressed nearly ever since the battles at Gettysburg, by what appeared to be evidences that your self, and Gen. Couch, and Gen. Smith, were not seeking a collision with the enemy, but were trying to get him across the river without another battle. What these evidences were, if you please, I hope to tell you at some time, when we shall both feel better. The case, summarily stated is this. You fought and beat the enemy at Gettysburg; and, of course, to say the least, his loss was as great as yours— He retreated; and you did not; as it seemed to me, pressingly pursue him; but a flood in the river detained him, till, by slow degrees, you were again upon him. You had at least twenty thousand veteran troops directly with you, and as many more raw ones within supporting distance, all in addition to those who fought with you at Gettysburg; while it was not possible that he had received a single recruit; and yet you stood and let the flood run down, bridges be built, and the enemy move away at his leisure, without attacking him. And Couch and Smith! The latter left Carlisle in time, upon all ordinary calculation, to have aided you in the last battle at Gettysburg; but he did not arrive— More At the end of more than ten days, I believe twelve, under constant urging, he reached Hagerstown from Carlisle, which is not an inch over fifty-five miles, if so much. And Couch's movement was very little different—

Again, my dear general, I do not believe you appreciate the magnitude of the misfortune involved in Lee's escape— He was within your easy grasp, and to have closed upon him would, in connection with the our other late successes, have ended the war— As it is, the war will be prolonged indefinitely. If you could not safely attack Lee last Monday, how can you possibly do so South of the river, when you can take with you very few more then two thirds of the force you then had in hand? It would be unreasonable to expect, and I do not expect you can now effect much. Your golden opportunity is gone, and I am distressed immeasurably because of it—

I beg you will not consider this a prosecution, or persecution of yourself— As you had learned that I was dissatisfied, I have thought it best to kindly tell you why.

Not signed

The Gettysburg Address

The dedication of the Soldiers' National Cemetery took place on November 19, 1863. The main speaker for the event was Edward Everett, a well-known orator and statesman of the time; however, President Lincoln was also asked to say a few words. Everett's speech lasted two hours; Lincoln's lasted two minutes. This is what Everett wrote to the President later on: "I wish that I could flatter myself that I had come as near to the central idea of the occasion in two hours as you did in two minutes."

There are five slightly different known drafts of the speech. Lincoln gave the first draft to his secretary, John G. Nicolay, and the second to his assistant, John Hay. The copy of the Gettysburg Address known as the Bliss Copy is the one most often reproduced. It is the version on display at the White House. Because the speech was not recorded, no one knows for sure which version was used at the event.

The handwritten copy given to John Nicolay—the earliest known draft—is shown on this page and the next. (For practical purposes, page 2 is shown on this page and page 1 on the next.)

Page 2

Executive Mansion.

Washington, _____ , 186 .

Four score and seven years ago our fathers brought forth, upon this continent, a new nation, conceived in liberty, and dedicated to the proposition that "all men are created equal"

Now we are engaged in a great civil war, testing whether that nation, or any nation so conceived, and so dedicated, can long endure. We are met on a great battle field of that war. We have come to dedicate a portion of it, as a final rest= ing place for those who died here, that the nation might live. This we may, in all propriety do. But, in a larger sense, we can not dedicate — we can not consecrate — we can not hallow, this ground — The brave men, living and dead, who struggled here, have hallowed it, far above our poor power to add or detract. The world will little note, nor long remember what we say here; while it can never forget what they did here.

It is rather for us, the living, to stand here, we here be dedica

Transcription of the Nicolay Copy

Executive Mansion,

Washington, , 186 .

Four score and seven years ago our fathers brought forth, upon this continent, a new nation, conceived in liberty, and dedicated to the proposition that "all men are created equal"

Now we are engaged in a great civil war, testing whether that nation, or any nation so conceived, and so dedicated, can long endure. We are met on a great battle field of that war. We have come to dedicate a portion of it, as a final resting place for those who died here, that the nation might live. This we may, in all propriety do. But, in a larger sense, we can not dedicate—we can not consecrate—we can not hallow, this ground—The brave men, living and dead, who struggled here, have hallowed it, far above our poor power to add or detract. The world will little note, nor long remember what we say here; while it can never forget what they did here.

It is rather for us, the living, to stand here, we here be dedicated to the great task remaining before us—that, from these honored dead we take increased devotion to that cause for which they here, gave the last full measure of devotion—that we here highly resolve these dead shall not have died in vain; that the nation, shall have a new birth of freedom, and that government of the people by the people for the people, shall not perish from the earth.

Transcription of the Bliss Copy

Four score and seven years ago our fathers brought forth on this continent, a new nation, conceived in Liberty, and dedicated to the proposition that all men are created equal.

Now we are engaged in a great civil war, testing whether that nation, or any nation so conceived and so dedicated, can long endure. We are met on a great battle-field of that war. We have come to dedicate a portion of that field, as a final resting place for those who here gave their lives that nation might live. It is altogether fitting and proper that we should do this.

But, in a larger sense, we can not dedicate—we can not consecrate—we can not hallow—this ground. The brave men, living and dead, who struggled here, have consecrated it, far above our poor power to add or detract. The world will little note, nor long remember what we say here, but it can never forget what they did here. It is for us the living, rather, to be dedicated here to the unfinished work which they who fought here have thus far so nobly advanced. It is rather for us to be here dedicated to the great task remaining before us—that from these honored dead we take increased devotion to that cause for which they gave the last full measure of devotion—that we here highly resolve that these dead shall not have died in vain—that this nation, under God, shall have a new birth of freedom—and that government of the people, by the people, for the people, shall not perish from the earth.

Think About It

1. Read the transcriptions of the Nicolay and Bliss copies. What is the most significant change?

2. Summarize the main reason for the gathering.

3. Were both Union and Confederate soldiers being buried in the Soldiers' National Cemetery? How do you know?

4. What was the "great task" Lincoln referred to?

5. Some words were taken from another important American document. Explain.

6. Look up the definition of any word you are unsure of. On another sheet of paper, rewrite the speech in your own words.

7. Why, do you think, did Lincoln underline the word "did" in the sentence beginning "The world will little note"?

8. Many people believe that presenting things in threes can make a speech more effective. Find examples of President Lincoln's use of the "Rule of Three" when writing this speech.

9. According to Lincoln, what was the job of the living?

The Election of 1864

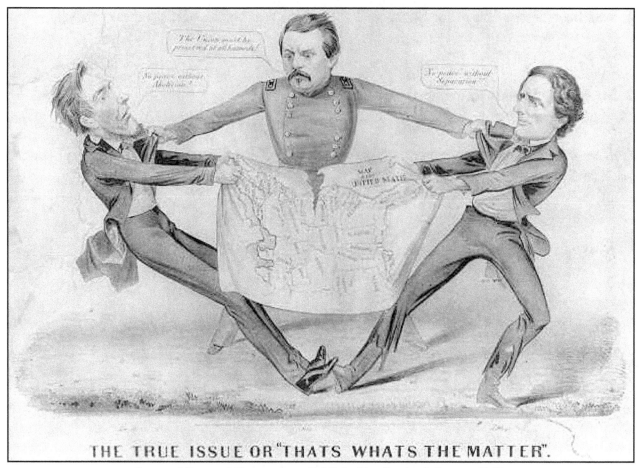

Source: Library of Congress   Published by Currier & Ives, c. 1864.

"The True Issue or 'That's What's the Matter' "

In this political cartoon, President Abraham Lincoln and Jefferson Davis, President of the Confederacy, are having a tug of war. General McClellan, Lincoln's opponent in the election of 1864, is in the middle. The following is written in the speech bubbles:

- "The Union must be preserved at all hazards!"
- "No peace without abolition."
- "No peace without Separation!!"

Think About It

1. What are Lincoln and Davis pulling on?

2. What is happening to the object they are pulling on as a result?

3. Who is saying what?

© **Barbara M. Peller**

4. How is McClellan portrayed? What does that tell us about what McClellan might have done to end the war if he had won the election?

"Grand, National Union Banner for 1864"

Think About It

1. What type of poster is this?

2. Why are Abraham Lincoln and Andrew Johnson featured on the poster?

3. What feelings is the poster meant to evoke? What images help evoke those feelings?

Source: Library of Congress's Prints and Photographs Division

Note: Original is in color. To view in color, use this url: https://www.loc.gov/pictures/resource/ppmsca.17562/

General Sherman's March to the Sea

Background Information

Maj. Gen. William Tecumseh Sherman began the military campaign that became known as Sherman's March to the Sea on November 15, 1864. Having captured Atlanta in September, Sherman decided to lead his army on a March to the Sea to Savannah. About 61,000 men would stay in northern Georgia and Tennessee; led by Maj. Gen. George H. Thompson, they would deal with the Confederates under General Lt. Gen. John Bell Hood. The other 62,000 would go with Sherman on his march towards Savannah, which was farther south and on the Atlantic coast.

Sherman did not have a supply train. Instead, he ordered his soldiers to take what they needed from the civilians they encountered along the way. The men took all they could carry and often burned what they could not.

As they advanced, the soldiers destroyed bridges, tunnels, and railroad tracks. They burned houses and barns. The men also pulled down telegraph lines.

Because the Confederates under Hood had to deal with the troops who stayed to the north, only a few thousand remained to fight against Sherman and his army of 62,000 men as they headed for Savannah. Most of the forces Sherman did encounter had too few men and were too weak to do any real damage.

Sherman captured Savannah, Georgia, on December 21, 1864.

Think About It

1. In the engraving on the following page, you can see two of the men trying to take down a telegraph pole. Why, do you suppose, would they want to do that?

2. Look at the portion of the engraving shown at the top of the next page. What are the men in the bottom right corner doing? Why, do you suppose, would they want to do that?

3. In general, why did Sherman order the destruction of bridges, railroads, and tunnels?

4. In general, why did he order the men to burn the houses and barns?

5. Evaluate the success of Sherman's destruction of military targets; infrastructure, such as bridges and tunnels; and civilian property.

This engraving by Alexander Hay Ritchie depicting Sherman's March to the Sea is shown in 2 parts because of size constraints.

Source:
Library of Congress

Using Primary Sources to Teach U.S. History: The American Civil War

Letter from President Lincoln to General Sherman: Transcription

December 26, 1864

"MY DEAR GENERAL SHERMAN: Many, many thanks for your Christmas gift, the capture of Savannah. When you were about leaving Atlanta for the Atlantic coast, I was anxious, if not fearful; but feeling that you were the better judge, and remembering that 'nothing risked, nothing gained,' I did not interfere. Now, the undertaking being a success, the honor is yours; for I believe none of us went further than to acquiesce. And taking the work of General Thomas into the county, as it should be taken, it is indeed a great success. Not only does it afford the obvious and immediate military advantages, but, in showing to the world that your army could be divided, putting the stronger part to an important new service, and yet leaving enough to vanquish the old opposing force of the whole—Hood's army—it brings those who sat in darkness to see a great light. But what next? I suppose it will be safer if I leave General Grant and yourself to decide. Please make my grateful acknowledgments to your whole army, officers and men."

Source: U.S. War Department

Think About It

1. The above letter was written by President Abraham Lincoln to General Sherman on December 26, 1864. It was in response to a letter that Sherman had sent to Lincoln on December 22. What, do you think, was the main idea of Sherman's letter to Lincoln?

2. Why didn't President Lincoln tell Sherman of his apprehensions when Sherman set out for Savannah?

3. Whom did President Lincoln credit for the success of the campaign? What does it tell us about the President?

4. How else did Lincoln show that he had faith in his generals?

© **Barbara M. Peller**

Mary Edwards Walker

Background Information

Mary Edwards Walker was the first female to be awarded the Medal of Honor (and as of this writing the only female). She was honored for her work as a surgeon during the Civil War.

Dr. Walker hoped to be a surgeon in the Army, but she was denied the appointment because of her gender. Unwilling to accept a position as a nurse, she instead worked unpaid in a temporary military hospital that had been set up in the U.S. Patent Office. She also volunteered to work in field hospitals in Virginia.

In September 1863 Dr. Walker was given a contract as an acting assistant surgeon. The position was equal in pay and authority to a lieutenant or captain. She briefly was regiment surgeon of the 53rd Ohio Infantry as well.

In April 1864 Dr. Walker was captured by the Confederates. Four months later she was released in a prisoner exchange.

Source: National Institutes of Health

Following her release, she was appointed medical director in a hospital for women prisoners in Louisville, Kentucky.

On November 11, 1865, President Andrew Johnson awarded Mary Walker the Medal of Honor. Unfortunately, her award—along with 910 others—was rescinded two years before her death. The

reason was a change in the standards. The new standards required "direct combat with an enemy." Federal marshals tried to take back the medal, but she refused to give it up and continued to wear it until she died. In 1977 President Carter reinstated the awards.

Think About It

1. What do you notice about the way Dr. Walker sometimes dressed? In your opinion, why did she dress this way?

2. Evaluate President Carter's decision to restore the medals to Dr. Walker and the others.

Photograph by C. M. Bell
Source: Library of Congress

The Fall of Richmond

Background Information

Richmond was not only the capital of Virginia but also the capital of the Confederate States of America. (It replaced Montgomery, Alabama, as capital of the Confederacy shortly after Virginia seceded.) The city was strategic, both politically and economically. Before the war, its most important industries were tobacco manufacturing and flour milling. Once the war was underway, however, the ironworks industries gained in importance. The Confederate Army was especially reliant on Tredegar Iron Works. Among the products they supplied were iron cladding for naval vessels, bullets, and buttons for the uniforms.

Once the war started, the population of Richmond grew by leaps and bounds. Overcrowding soon became a problem. Crime increased, epidemics of smallpox and other diseases spread, and food and fuel became scarce. The situation came to a head with the Richmond Bread Riot. A crowd, comprising about 5,000 women, broke into shops and stole food, clothing, and other items. The governor finally put a stop to the looting by calling on the state militia to restore order.

The people of Richmond also had to deal with the constant need to care for the sick and wounded soldiers who were brought to the city. The Confederate Congress standardized the hospital system and created a Confederate Medical Department. Chimborazo Hospital in Richmond became the largest in the Confederacy; it had one of the lowest mortality rates not only in the Confederacy but also in the Union.

From May 4 to June 12 General Grant carried out his Overland Campaign against General Lee in Virginia. This campaign resulted in huge numbers of wounded: 55,000 for the Union and 33,000 for the Confederacy. Grant was persistent. On June 12, he began a new campaign that would last more than nine months. His aim was to take the city of Richmond by going through Petersburg, which was only twenty-five miles from Richmond.

When nearby Petersburg fell to the Union, it became clear to General Lee that Richmond would have to be evacuated. On April 2, 1865, Lee notified Jefferson Davis that the city could not be defended and warned that it should be evacuated. Davis heeded his advice. He and his entire cabinet abandoned Richmond and fled south. So did many other Confederate supporters.

Before leaving Richmond, the Confederates set parts of the city on fire. They wanted to destroy anything that the Union troops might be able to use against the Confederates who remained. When the Union troops arrived, the city formally surrendered. The troops then extinguished the fires.

Richmond was the last important Confederate city to fall into the hands of the Union. Savannah, Charleston, and Atlanta were already under Union control following Sherman's March to the Sea. The War Between the States was nearing an end. About a week after the fall of Richmond, General Robert E. Lee would surrender to General Grant at Appomattox Court House.

"The Campaign in Virginia—On to Richmond"

Published by *Harper's Weekly*

"The Campaign in Virginia—On to Richmond"

Because of Richmond's strategic importance, many Union campaigns were aimed at the city. "On to Richmond!" became a popular battle cry. The above drawing, which was featured in the June 18 (backdated from June 8), 1864, issue of *Harper's Weekly*, was created by Thomas Nast.

Think About It

1. General Grant is in the illustration. Can you identify him?

2. What is the mood created by this illustration?

3. *Harper's Weekly*, which was published in New York, favored the Union side during the Civil War. How do you think its readers reacted to this picture?

Currier and Ives—"The Fall of Richmond, VA, on the Night of April 2, 1865" (cropped)
The original lithograph is in color. To view the image in full color, use the following url:
https://commons.wikimedia.org/wiki/File:Currier_and_Ives_-
_The_Fall_of_Richmond,_Va._on_the_Night_of_April_2d._1865_(cropped).jpg

View of Richmond above the Canal Basin, after the Evacuation Fire of 1865
National Archives

© **Barbara M. Peller**

Think About It

1. Describe the scene in the lithograph entitled "Fall of Richmond" (top visual on the previous page).

2. Identify the columned building located to the right of the fires.

3. Describe the scene in the bottom visual on the previous page. What can we learn about the columned building identified in Number 2 above?

4. What can we infer from the photo below?

Photo by Photographer from Mathew Brady's Outfit (cropped)
National Archives

Surrender at Appomattox Court House

Background Information

With the Confederate evacuation of Richmond, things were looking bleak for General Lee's Army of Northern Virginia. On April 7, 1865, General Grant wrote to General Lee asking if he was ready to surrender. Lee did not immediately accept, but after a few more setbacks, he realized the futility of continuing his resistance and sent word that he would surrender.

The surrender took place at the home of William McLean in the small village of Appomattox Court House, Virginia, on April 9, 1865. Lee arrived around 1:00 p.m. Grant arrived about thirty minutes later. They agreed to meet again the next day to work out the details. That meeting would comprise six officers, three from each side.

The following issues were discussed and agreed upon:

- The soldiers would be given printed passes to prove they were paroled prisoners.

- Confederates who had to pass through Union-controlled territories would be provided with free transportation on the U.S. government's railroads and vessels.

- Confederate cavalrymen and artillerymen would be allowed to keep their horses.

- The Confederates would be supplied with 25,000 rations. (Most of these had been obtained when Union troops under Major General Philip Sheridan seized the Confederate supply train at Appomattox.)

Although the surrender at Appomattox Court House was an important step towards peace, and future Confederate surrenders would be modeled on it, it did not end the war. In fact, the War Between the States would not officially come to a close until August 20, 1866—more than sixteen months later. On that date President Johnson—Abraham Lincoln had been assassinated by then—issued the following proclamation:

> *"And I do further proclaim that the said insurrection is at an end and that peace, order, tranquility, and civil authority now exists in and throughout the whole of the United States of America."*

Jefferson Davis was captured near Irwinville, Georgia, on May 10, 1865, having fled from the Union Army after he and his cabinet evacuated Richmond. His plan was to make his way to Florida and escape by sea to Texas, where he hoped to form a new Confederacy.

"The Room in the McLean House…"

The line below the image of the lithograph shown on the next page reads as follows: "Appomattox C.H., in which Gen. Lee surrendered to Gen. Grant." Grant and Lee are seen waiting for the terms of the peace agreement to be copied.

Source: Library of Congress

"The Room in the McLean House, in Appomattox C.H. , in which GEN. LEE surrendered to GEN. GRANT"

Pictured Left to Right: John Gibbon, George Armstrong Custer, Cyrus B. Comstock, Orville E. Babcock, Charles Marshall, Walter H. Taylor, Robert E. Lee, Philip Sheridan, Ulysses S. Grant, John Aaron Rawlins, Charles Griffin, unidentified, George Meade, Ely S. Parker, James W. Forsyth, Wesley Merritt, Theodore Shelton Bowers, Edward Ord. The man not identified is thought to be General Joshua Chamberlain, who presided over the formal surrender of arms by Lee's Army of Northern Virginia.

Think About It

1. Compare the demeanors of Grant and Lee. Cite reasons for your opinion.

2. The agreement between General Grant and General Lee is often referred to as a "Gentlemen's Agreement." Evaluate the appropriateness of that term.

Andersonville Prison

Background Information

Built in 1864 and officially named Camp Sumter, the military prison in Andersonville, Georgia, was infamous for its harsh conditions and mistreatment of prisoners. During the last fourteen months of the war, more than 45,000 Union soldiers were imprisoned there; about 13,000 of them died. At one time there were as many as 33,000 prisoners in a space designed for 10,000. This over-crowding was a major contributor to the horrid conditions and high mortality rate.

Overcrowding had many dire consequences. Some prisoners died of exposure due to the lack of clothing. Many died from starvation. Others died from scurvy, caused by a lack of vitamin C. The extremely poor sanitary conditions led to outbreaks of other diseases. Among the most serious were dysentery, hookworms, and typhoid. One of the main causes of disease was the fact that the main source of water for the prisoners was a contaminated creek that ran through the prison camp.

A stockade comprising an inner stockade, a second-line stockade, and a third-line stockade surrounded the camp. Sentry boxes, referred to as pigeon roosts, were set up at intervals; armed guards were in each box. In order to prevent prisoners from attempting to climb the stockade walls, a "dead line" was erected about 19 feet in from the wall. It was really just a simple fence. If a prisoner was seen trying to go past it, he was immediately shot.

The remaining prisoners at Andersonville were liberated in May 1865. People were horrified to see their emaciated bodies. Henry Wirz, commander of the inner stockade, was tried and convicted of war crimes.

Think About It

Both of the photos on the next page were taken on August 17, 1864.

1. Describe what you see in the top photo.

2. Can you guess what is happening?

3. The photo on the bottom is the southwest view of stockade. Describe what you see.

Source: Library of Congress

Source: Library of Congress

The Assassination of President Lincoln

Background Information

President Lincoln was assassinated by John Wilkes Booth on April 14, 1865, only five days after General Lee surrendered to General Grant at Appomattox Court House, Virginia.

Booth was a well known actor. Although a Confederate sympathizer, he lived in the North throughout the Civil War. His original plan was to kidnap President Lincoln and bring him to Richmond, but that did not work out and became impossible after the fall of Richmond.

When Booth found out that the President and his wife would be attending a performance at Ford's Theatre, he devised a new plan. He would assassinate President Lincoln, and his co-conspirators would kill Vice President Andrew Johnson and Secretary of State William H. Seward. He hypothesized that this would send the government into disarray and save the Confederacy.

Photo by Alexander Gardner
Source: Library of Congress

When Lincoln's bodyguard left his post, Booth took advantage of the opportunity to attack. At 10:15 in the evening, Booth entered the box occupied by Lincoln and his party and fired a shot, hitting the President in the head. He then jumped onto the stage and yelled, *"Sic semper tyrannis!"* It means "Thus ever to tyrants" and is the Virginia state motto.

Some soldiers carried the President to a nearby boardinghouse and waited for the surgeon general. The surgeon general concluded that nothing could be done, and Lincoln died the following morning.

The nation mourned! As they did, a massive manhunt began for the assassin and his co-conspirators. On April 26 a sergeant shot and killed John Wilkes Booth, allegedly after Booth pulled his gun first. Four co-conspirators were eventually convicted and hanged. Among them were David Herold and Mary Surratt, the first woman to be executed by the U.S. government. Not only had Mary Surratt allowed the conspirators to use her boardinghouse to devise their plan, she also left weapons for them to aid in their escape.

PORTION OF THE WANTED POSTER: TRANSCRIPTION

LIBERAL REWARDS will be paid for any information that shall conduce to the arrest of either of the above-named criminals, or their accomplices.

All persons harboring or secreting the said persons, or either of them, or aiding or assisting their concealment or escape, will be treated as accomplices in the murder of the President and the attempted assassination of the Secretary of State, and shall be subject to trial before a Military Commission and the punishment of DEATH.

Let the stain of innocent blood be removed from the land by the arrest and punishment of the murderers.

All good citizens are exhorted to aid public justice on this occasion. Every man should consider his own conscience charged with this solemn duty, and rest neither night nor day until it be accomplished.

Think About It

1. Explain the purpose of this document.

2. Why, do you think, did Booth believe that killing Johnson and Seward would throw the government into disarray?

3. Who are the people shown at the top?

4. Who was offering the reward? What was the breakdown of the $100,000 being offered?

5. Research and find out why the attempted assassination of the Secretary of State is mentioned but not that of the Vice President.

6. According to the poster, what will be the punishment for the murderer and his accomplices if found guilty by the Military Commission?

7. According to the poster, how could the pain caused by the President's assassination be alleviated?

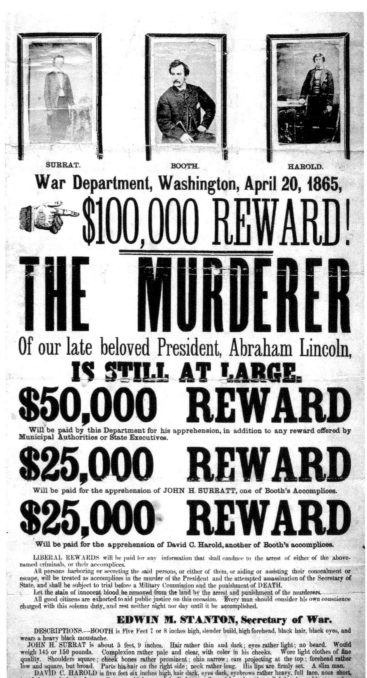

Source: Library of Congress

8. What is at the bottom of the poster following Stanton's name and title?

Civil War Music

Background Information

Music played an important role during the Civil War both in the North and in the South. As part of the day-to-day life of the soldiers, music provided much more than entertainment. It also helped to calm soldiers before and after battle and provided motivation during the battle. Patriotic songs helped boost the morale of the soldiers and raised the spirits of those they left behind. They also helped to create a feeling of national identity. This was especially important for the Confederacy.

Sheet music was very popular. Most were sold as booklets with illustrated covers, often battle scenes. "The Battle Cry for Freedom," considered by many to be the most popular song among the Union soldiers, was created by George F. Root in response to President Lincoln's call for 300,000 volunteers. The response to the song was immense. Between 500,000 and 700,000 copies of the song were printed.

Both drums and bugles were crucial communication tools. The infantry used drums to wake the soldiers and to inform them where to report. Drummers played "taps" at night to tell the soldiers when to go to sleep. Officers used the rhythms of the drums in battle to convey orders to the troops. The cavalry and artillery units used bugles instead of drums to perform similar functions.

When the fighting started, the drummers were often sent to the rear to assist the medical personnel. Sometimes, however, they remained in the middle of the battle. Their patriotic and fighting songs motivated the soldiers. Hymns and songs about the life they left behind encouraged them once the fighting stopped. Fifers often played alongside the drummers.

Music was also important to those remaining on the home front. Regimental bands played patriotic tunes at rallies to boost support. They also played soothing ballads to allay the fears of those left behind.

The following were some of the most popular songs. The lyrics to these songs can be found on pages 90–93.

Union Civil War Songs
- Battle Cry of Freedom
- Battle Hymn Of The Republic
- We Are Coming Father Abraham
- Tramp, Tramp, Tramp

Confederate Civil War Songs
- The Bonnie Blue Flag
- Dixie's Land
- God Save the South
- Goober Peas

Young Drummer Boy
for 78th Colored Troops Infantry
Source: Library of Congress

Source: Library of Congress

"The Songs of War"

This print was created by the artist Winslow Homer and published in *Harper's Weekly* on November 23, 1861. The seven songs depicted in the illustration are "The Bold Soldier Boy," "Battle Hymn of the Republic," "Dixie," "Hail to the Chief," "We'll Be Free and Easy Still," "Rogue's March," and "The Girl I Left Behind." Each scene represents a different song and different facet of the war. At the time of the Civil War, the people would have been aware of which songs the scenes were linked to.

Think About It

1. See if you can figure out which song is represented by each scene.

2. "Dixie" was a battle cry of the South. Why, do you think, did Winslow Homer include it?

"Grafted into the Army," *by Henry Clay Work*

"Grafted into the Army," by Henry Clay Work, was written as a protest to the draft acts. At the start of the war there were enough volunteers to meet the needs of the military in both the North and the South. With time, however, that changed. The Confederates were the first to feel the need to enact a draft. They did so on April 16, 1862. The act mandated that all white males between the ages of 18 and 35 (later 45) enlist for three years of service. The following March, the Federal government passed a similar act. Called the Enrollment Act, it required the enlistment of men between 20 and 45.

Both the Confederate act and the Union act allowed a draftee either to have a substitute serve on his behalf or to pay a $300 exemption fee.

Grafted into the Army

Our Jimmy has gone for to live in a tent,
   They have grafted him into the army;
He finally pucker'd up his courage and went,
   When they grafted him into the army.
 I told them he was too young, alas!
   At the captain's forequarters, they said he would pass.
They'd train him up well in the infantry class—
   So they grafted him into the army.

CHORUS:
Oh, Jimmy, farewell! Your brothers fell
   Way down in Alabarmy;
I thought they would spare a lone widder's heir,
   But they grafted him into the army.

Drest up in his unicorn—dear little chap;
   They have grafted him into the army;
It seems but a day since he sot in my lap,
   But they grafted him into the army.
And these are the trousers he used to wear—
   Them very same buttons—the patch and the tear—
But Uncle Sam gave him a bran'new pair
   When they grafted him into the army.—CHORUS

Sheet Music Cover
for "Grafted into the Army"

Now in my provisions I see him revealed—
   They have grafted him into the army;
A picket beside the contented field.
   They have grafted him into the army.
He looks kinda sickish—begins to cry—
   A big volunteer standing right in his eye!
On, what if the ducky should up and die
   Now they've grafted him into the army.—CHORUS

Think About It: "Grafted into the Army,"

1. Explain the pun on which this song is based.

2. Why did many people protest these acts?

3. Summarize the story told by this song.

4. What is the woman on the cover of the sheet music holding in her hand? What does the image on the bottom represent?

Sheet Music Cover
for "The Bonnie Blue Flag"
Note: Original is in color.

Think About It: "The Bonnie Blue Flag," by Harry McCarthy

1. The image above is of the cover of the sheet music for the song "The Bonnie Blue Flag." Read the lyrics found on page 92 and describe in one sentence the story told by the song.

2. General Butler, who ruled over New Orleans when the Union occupied the city, issued an order (General Order No. 40) that made singing or owning the song "The Bonnie Blue Flag" an act of treason. Use the definition of treason as stated in Article III, Section 3, of the Constitution to evaluate that order.

Think About It: "Tramp, Tramp, Tramp," by George F. Root

1. Read the lyrics of "Tramp, Tramp, Tramp" found on page 90. From whose point of view is it written?

Reconstruction Amendments

Background Information

The period following the American Civil War was known as the Reconstruction Era. It lasted from 1865 to 1877. The South's railroads, factories, bridges, and plantations were in ruin and had to be restored. Also, problems dealing with the states' re-entry into the Union had to be resolved. Recent enemies, the North and the South now had to work together.

President Lincoln's plan said that he would pardon or offer amnesty to any Southerner who pledged loyalty to the United States with the exception of high-ranking officers and political leaders. He agreed to readmit states into the Union when ten percent of their voting population of 1860 had taken that oath of allegiance. Lincoln also said that he would protect their property except, of course, for their slaves.

When President Lincoln was assassinated on April 15, 1865, President Johnson took over. At first his plan seemed harsh against the southern aristocracy. Civil and military officers of the Confederacy were disenfranchised. Estates worth more than $20,000 were confiscated. Some of that land was then distributed to freed slaves by the Freedmen's Bureau. However, President Johnson soon reversed most of that. He issued many pardons and gave back much of the land to the white landowners. In order to be readmitted to the Union, the states had to ratify the Thirteenth Amendment, which abolished slavery. However, laws known as black codes were enacted; these laws greatly limited the freedom and rights of the blacks.

Reconstruction Amendments

Republicans took office in Congress in the 1866 election, and Congress passed three important Reconstruction Amendments. The Thirteenth Amendment was ratified in 1865; the Fourteenth Amendment was ratified in 1868; and the Fifteenth Amendment was ratified in 1870.

Think About It

1. Read the Reconstruction Amendments on the next page. What do they have in common?

2. Create a one-sentence summary for each of the three amendments.

3. A portion of the Fourteenth Amendment was later changed by the Twenty-sixth Amendment. Explain.

© **Barbara M. Peller**

Reconstruction Amendments

Amendment XIII

SECTION. 1. Neither slavery nor involuntary servitude, except as a punishment for crime whereof the party shall have been duly convicted, shall exist within the United States, or any place subject to their jurisdiction.

SECTION. 2. Congress shall have power to enforce this article by appropriate legislation.

Amendment XIV

SECTION. 1. All persons born or naturalized in the United States, and subject to the jurisdiction thereof, are citizens of the United States and of the State wherein they reside. No State shall make or enforce any law which shall abridge the privileges or immunities of citizens of the United States; nor shall any State deprive any person of life, liberty, or property, without due process of law; nor deny to any person within its jurisdiction the equal protection of the laws.

SECTION. 2. Representatives shall be apportioned among the several States according to their respective numbers, counting the whole number of persons in each State, excluding Indians not taxed. But when the right to vote at any election for the choice of electors for President and Vice-President of the United States, Representatives in Congress, the Executive and Judicial officers of a State, or the members of the Legislature thereof, is denied to any of the male inhabitants of such State, being twenty-one years of age, and citizens of the United States, or in any way abridged, except for participation in rebellion, or other crime, the basis of representation therein shall be reduced in the proportion which the number of such male citizens shall bear to the whole number of male citizens twenty-one years of age in such State.

SECTION. 3. No person shall be a Senator or Representative in Congress, or elector of President and Vice-President, or hold any office, civil or military, under the United States, or under any State, who, having previously taken an oath, as a member of Congress, or as an officer of the United States, or as a member of any State legislature, or as an executive or judicial officer of any State, to support the Constitution of the United States, shall have engaged in insurrection or rebellion against the same, or given aid or comfort to the enemies thereof. But Congress may by a vote of two-thirds of each House, remove such disability.

SECTION. 4. The validity of the public debt of the United States, authorized by law, including debts incurred for payment of pensions and bounties for services in suppressing insurrection or rebellion, shall not be questioned. But neither the United States nor any State shall assume or pay any debt or obligation incurred in aid of insurrection or rebellion against the United States, or any claim for the loss or emancipation of any slave; but all such debts, obligations and claims shall be held illegal and void.

SECTION. 5. The Congress shall have the power to enforce, by appropriate legislation, the provisions of this article.

Amendment XV

SECTION. 1. The right of citizens of the United States to vote shall not be denied or abridged by the United States or by any State on account of race, color, or previous condition of servitude.

SECTION. 2. The Congress shall have the power to enforce this article by appropriate legislation.

Popular Civil War Songs

Battle Hymn of the Republic,
by Julia W. Howe

Mine eyes have seen the glory of the coming of the Lord;
He is trampling out the vintage where the grapes of wrath
    are stored;
He hath loosed the fateful lightning of His terrible swift sword;
His truth is marching on.
Glory! Glory! Hallelujah! Glory! Glory! Hallelujah!
Glory! Glory! Hallelujah! His truth is marching on.

I have seen Him in the watch fires of a hundred circling camps
They have builded Him an altar in the evening dews and damps;
I can read His righteous sentence by the dim and flaring lamps;
His day is marching on.
Glory! Glory! Hallelujah! Glory! Glory! Hallelujah!
Glory! Glory! Hallelujah! His day is marching on.

I have read a fiery Gospel writ in burnished rows of steel;
"As ye deal with My contemners, so with you My grace
    shall deal";
Let the Hero, born of woman, crush the serpent with His heel,
Since God is marching on.
Glory! Glory! Hallelujah! Glory! Glory! Hallelujah!
Glory! Glory! Hallelujah! Since God is marching on.

He has sounded forth the trumpet that shall never call retreat;
He is sifting out the hearts of men before His judgment seat;
Oh, be swift, my soul, to answer Him! be jubilant, my feet;
Our God is marching on.
Glory! Glory! Hallelujah! Glory! Glory! Hallelujah!
Glory! Glory! Hallelujah! Our God is marching on.

In the beauty of the lilies Christ was born across the sea,
With a glory in His bosom that transfigures you and me:
As He died to make men holy, let us live to make men free;
[originally ...let us die to make men free]
While God is marching on.
Glory! Glory! Hallelujah! Glory! Glory! Hallelujah!
Glory! Glory! Hallelujah! While God is marching on.

He is coming like the glory of the morning on the wave,
He is wisdom to the mighty, He is honor to the brave;
So the world shall be His footstool, and the soul of wrong
    His slave,
Our God is marching on.
Glory! Glory! Hallelujah! Glory! Glory! Hallelujah!
Glory! Glory! Hallelujah! Our God is marching on.

Battle Cry of Freedom, *by George F. Root*

Yes, we'll rally round the flag, boys, we'll rally once again,
Shouting the battle cry of freedom,
We will rally from the hillside, we'll gather from the plain,
Shouting the battle cry of freedom!

CHORUS:
The Union forever! Hurrah, boys, hurrah!
Down with the traitor, up with the star;
While we rally round the flag, boys, rally once again,
Shouting the battle cry of freedom!

We are springing to the call with a million freemen more,
Shouting the battle cry of freedom!
And we'll fill our vacant ranks of our brothers gone before,
Shouting the battle cry of freedom!—CHORUS

We will welcome to our numbers the loyal, true and brave,
Shouting the battle cry of freedom!
And although he may be poor, he shall never be a slave,
Shouting the battle cry of freedom!—CHORUS

So we're springing to the call from the East and from the West,
Shouting the battle cry of freedom!
And we'll hurl the rebel crew from the land we love best,
Shouting the battle cry of freedom!—CHORUS

Tramp, Tramp, Tramp, *by George F. Root*

In the prison cell I sit, thinking mother, dear, of you and our bright and happy home so far away. And the tears they fill my eyes, in spite of all that I can do, though I try to cheer my comrades and be gay.

CHORUS: Tramp, tramp, tramp. The boys are marching. Cheer up, comrades, they will come. And beneath the starry flag, we shall breathe the air again, of the free land in our own beloved homes.

In the battle front we stood, when their fiercest charge they made, and they swept us off, a hundred men or more. But before they reached our lines, they were beaten back, dismayed. And we heard the cry of victory o'er and o'er.

—CHORUS

So within the prison cell, we are waiting for the day, that you'll come to open wide the iron door. And the hollow eye grow bright and the poor heart almost gay, when we think of seeing home and friends once more.
—CHORUS

We Are Coming, Father Abraham,
by James Sloan Gibbons

We are coming, Father Abraham, 300,000 more,
From Mississippi's winding stream and from
    New England's shore.
We leave our plows and workshops, our wives and
    children dear,
With hearts too full for utterance, with but a silent tear.
We dare not look behind us but steadfastly before.
We are coming, Father Abraham, 300,000 more!

CHORUS:
We are coming, we are coming our Union to restore,
We are coming, Father Abraham, 300,000 more!

If you look across the hilltops that meet the northern sky,
Long moving lines of rising dust your vision may descry;
And now the wind, an instant, tears the cloudy veil aside,
And floats aloft our spangled flag in glory and in pride;
And bayonets in the sunlight gleam, and bands brave
    music pour,
We are coming, father Abr'am, three hundred thousand
    more!—CHORUS

If you look up all our valleys where the growing
    harvests shine,
You may see our sturdy farmer boys fast forming into line;
And children from their mother's knees are pulling
    at the weeds ,
And learning how to reap and sow against their
    country's needs;
And a farewell group stands weeping at every cottage door,
We are coming, Father Abr'am, three hundred thousand
    more!—CHORUS

You have called us, and we're coming by Richmond's
    bloody tide,
To lay us down for freedom's sake, our brothers' bones
    beside;
Or from foul treason's savage group, to wrench the
    murderous blade;
And in the face of foreign foes its fragments to parade.
Six hundred thousand loyal men and true have gone
    before,
We are coming, Father Abraham, 300,000 more!
—CHORUS

God Save the South *by George H. Miles*

God save the South, God save the South,
Her altars and firesides, God save the South!
Now that the war is nigh, now that we arm to die,
Chanting our battle cry, "Freedom or death!"
Chanting our battle cry, "Freedom or death!"

God be our shield, at home or afield,
Stretch Thine arm over us, strengthen and save.
What tho' they're three to one, forward each sire and son,
Strike till the war is won, strike to the grave!
Strike till the war is won, strike to the grave!

God made the right stronger than might,
Millions would trample us down in their pride.
Lay Thou their legions low, roll back the ruthless foe,
Let the proud spoiler know God's on our side.
Let the proud spoiler know God's on our side.

Hark honor's call, summoning all.
Summoning all of us unto the strife.
Sons of the South, awake! Strike till the brand shall break,
Strike for dear Honor's sake, Freedom and Life!
Strike for dear Honor's sake, Freedom and Life!

Rebels before, our fathers of yore.
Rebel's the righteous name Washington bore.
Why, then, be ours the same, the name that he snatched
    from shame,
Making it first in fame, foremost in war.
Making it first in fame, foremost in war.

War to the hilt, theirs be the guilt,
Who fetter the free man to ransom the slave.
Up then, and undismay'd, sheathe not the battle blade,
Till the last foe is laid low in the grave!
Till the last foe is laid low in the grave!

God save the South, God save the South,
Dry the dim eyes that now follow our path.
Still let the light feet rove safe through the orange grove,
Still keep the land we love safe from Thy wrath.
Still keep the land we love safe from Thy wrath.

God save the South, God save the South,
Her altars and firesides, God save the South!
For the great war is nigh, and we will win or die,
Chanting our battle cry, "Freedom or death!"
Chanting our battle cry, "Freedom or death!"

The Bonnie Blue Flag, *by Harry McCarthy*

We are a band of brothers
And native to the soil,
Fighting for the property
We gained by honest toil;
And when our rights were threatened,
The cry rose near and far--
"Hurrah for the Bonnie Blue Flag
That bears a single star!"

CHORUS:
Hurrah! Hurrah!
For Southern rights hurrah!
Hurrah for the Bonnie Blue Flag
That bears a single star.

As long as the Union
Was faithful to her trust,
Like friends and like brothers
Both kind were we and just;
But now, when Northern treachery
Attempts our rights to mar,
We hoist on high the Bonnie Blue Flag
That bears a single star.—CHORUS

First gallant South Carolina
Nobly made the stand,
Then came Alabama,
Who took her by the hand.
Next quickly Mississippi,
Georgia and Florida
All raised on high the Bonnie Blue Flag
That bears a single star.—CHORUS

Ye men of valor, gather round
The banner of the right;
Texas and fair Louisiana
Join us in the fight.
Davis, our loved president,
And Stephens statesmen are;
Now rally round the Bonnie Blue Flag
That bears a single star.—CHORUS

And here's to old Virginia--
The Old Dominion State--
Who with the young Confederacy
At length has linked her fate;
Impelled by her example,
Now other states prepare
To hoist on high the Bonnie Blue Flag
That bears a single star.—CHORUS

Then cheer, boys, cheer;
Raise the joyous shout,
For Arkansas and North Carolina
Now have both gone out;
And let another rousing cheer
For Tennessee be given,
The single star of the Bonnie Blue Flag
Has grown to be eleven.—CHORUS

Then here's to our Confederacy,
Strong are we and brave;
Like patriots of old we'll fight
Our heritage to save.
And rather than submit to shame,
To die we would prefer;
So cheer for the Bonnie Blue Flag
That bears a single star.—CHORUS

Dixie's Land, *by Daniel Decatur Emmett*

I wish I was in the land of cotton,
Old times there are not forgotten;
    Look away! Look away! Look away, Dixie's Land!
In Dixie's Land where I was born in,
Early on one frosty morning,
    Look away! Look away! Look away, Dixie's Land!

CHORUS:
Then I wish I was in Dixie! Hooray! Hooray!
In Dixie's Land I'll take my stand, to live and die in Dixie!
Away! Away! Away down South in Dixie!
Away! Away! Away down South in Dixie!

Old Missus married "Will the Weaver";
William was a gay deceiver!
    Look away! Look away! Look away, Dixie's Land!
But when he put his arm around her,
Smiled as fierce as a forty-pounder!
    Look away! Look away! Look away, Dixie's Land!
—CHORUS

His face was sharp as a butcher's cleaver;
But that did not seem to grieve her!
    Look away! Look away! Look away, Dixie's Land!
Old Missus acted the foolish part
And died for a man that broke her heart!
    Look away! Look away! Look away, Dixie's Land!
—CHORUS

Now here's a health to the next old missus
And all the gals that want to kiss us!
    Look away! Look away! Look away, Dixie's Land!
But if you want to drive away sorrow,
Come and hear this song tomorrow!
    Look away! Look away! Look away, Dixie's Land!
—CHORUS

There's buckwheat cakes and Injin batter,
Makes you fat or a little fatter!
    Look away! Look away! Look away, Dixie's Land!
Then hoe it down and scratch your gravel,
To Dixie's Land I'm bound to travel!
    Look away! Look away! Look away, Dixie's Land!
—CHORUS

NOTE: There are many variations.

Humorous Songs

Singing songs—especially humorous ones—helped to pass the time and to relieve the tensions and stress of war. This silly song about goober peas, or peanuts, is an example of one of those songs.

Goober Peas, *by James Ryder Randall*

Stting by the roadside on a summer's day
Chatting with my mess-mates, passing time away
Lying in the shadows underneath the trees
Goodness, how delicious, eating goober peas.

Peas, peas, peas, peas
Eating goober peas
Goodness, how delicious,
Eating goober peas.

When a horse-man passes, the soldiers have a rule
To cry out their loudest, "Mister, here's your mule!"
But another custom, enchanting-er than these
Is wearing out your grinders, eating goober peas.

Peas, peas, peas, peas
Eating goober peas
Goodness, how delicious,
Eating goober peas.
Just before the battle, the General hears a row
He says "The Yanks are coming, I hear their rifles now."
He looks down the roadway, and what d'ya think he sees?
The Georgia Militia cracking goober peas.

Peas, peas, peas, peas
Eating goober peas
Goodness, how delicious,
Eating goober peas.

I think my song has lasted just about enough.
The subject is interesting, but the rhymes are mighty rough.
I wish the war was over, so free from rags and fleas.
We'd kiss our wives and sweethearts, say good-bye to
    goober peas.

Peas, peas, peas, peas
Eating goober peas
Goodness, how delicious,
Eating goober peas.

Suggested Answers

Missouri Compromise

1. What did Maine have to do before it could be admitted to the Union? Why?

Because it had to be an independent state before it could be admitted to the Union, Maine first had to get the consent of the legislature of Massachusetts to break away from that state.

2. What portion of the excerpt shows that Missouri retained the right to have slavery when it was admitted to the Union as a state?

The following gave Missouri the right to enter as a slave state: "…and the said state, when formed, shall be admitted into the Union, upon an equal footing with the original states, in all respects whatsoever."

3. What portion of the excerpt prohibited slavery in most areas ceded by France to the United States as part of the Louisiana Purchase? Underline the words that explain the exception.

"And be it further enacted. That in all that territory ceded by France to the United States, under the name of Louisiana, which lies north of thirty-six degrees and thirty minutes north latitude, <u>not included within the limits of the state, contemplated by this act,</u> slavery and involuntary servitude, otherwise than in the punishment of crimes, whereof the parties shall have been duly convicted, shall be, and is hereby, forever prohibited."

4. What portion upheld the Fugitive Slave Act?

The following upheld the Fugitive Slave Act: "Provided always, That any person escaping into the same, from whom labour or service is lawfully claimed, in any state or territory of the United States, such fugitive may be lawfully reclaimed and conveyed to the person claiming his or her labour or service as aforesaid."

Jefferson's Letter to Holmes

1. To what was Jefferson referring when he wrote the following: "…this momentous question, like a fire bell in the night, awakened and filled me with terror. I considered it at once as the knell of the Union"?

It referred to the Missouri Compromise, which terrified him because he feared that it would mean the end of the Union.

2. What aspect of the tensions bothered Jefferson the most?

It worried him that the sides were drawn around geographical lines. Previously divisions were around party lines, but since each state had both parties, this did not worry him as much.

3. Explain Jefferson's use of the idiom "to have a wolf by an ear" in the following excerpt: "But, as it is, we have the wolf by the ear, and we can neither hold him, nor safely let him go. Justice is in one scale, and self-preservation in the other."

It means to be in a precarious situation. He believed that justice called for emancipation, but he feared that emancipation would lead to the end of the Union.

4. Judge Jefferson's view that the Missouri Compromise was "a reprieve only, not a final sentence."

He was right. In 1860, the Confederate States would secede and civil war would follow.

5. How did Jefferson view the generation then in power?

He looked down upon them. He thought they were throwing away the gain that had been made by the founders.

The Compromise of 1850

1. Can you find Clay, Webster, and Calhoun in the image entitled "The United States Senate, A.D. 1850"?

Clay is the one giving the speech. He is presenting his proposal of the laws that came to be known as the Compromise of 1850. Webster is seated to his left with his head leaning on his hand. Calhoun is third from the right.

2. Whom does Clay seem to be addressing? How do you know?

He is addressing Vice President Millard Fillmore. As vice president, Fillmore presided over the Senate during these debates.

Ralph Waldo Emerson

1. Analyze the Ralph Waldo Emerson's quotation about slavery.

Answers will vary.

2. How did Emerson's views of Webster change? Why?

In 1834 he admired Webster and thought that he was a leader advocating freedom for all. In 1851 he thought that Webster had betrayed his principles by speaking in favor of the Compromise of 1850 instead of advocating for abolition.

The Fugitive Slave Law

1. Garrison is pointing his gun at the man on Webster's back. Who, do you think, is that man? How do you know?

It is a slave catcher. The man is holding a noose and manacles.

2. Webster is holding a copy of the Constitution. Based upon this cartoon, how do you think Webster felt about enforcing the Fugitive Slave Law?

He believed it should be enforced because it was constitutional, but he did not like having to do it.

3. On which side do you think the artist was? Cite examples.

The artist was opposed to the Fugitive Slave Law. The Temple of Liberty in the background is flying two flags. One says, "A day, an hour, of virtuous Liberty, is worth an age of Servitude." The other says, "All men are born free & equal."

4. The fallen slaveholder blames Webster for his downfall. Why might he have been to blame?
Webster supported the Compromise of 1850 after the passage of the Fugitive Slave Act, which in some ways restricted slavery. Also, after the Compromise, abolitionists became more resolved to end slavery. The nation became more aware of the issue and many who hadn't given it much thought now took a strong stance against the institution.

Poster: "Caution!! Colored People of Boston"
1. What was the purpose of this poster?
The purpose was to warn fugitive slaves to stay clear of police officers and watchmen.
2. Why was the warning necessary?
The officers had been employed to catch the slaves having been given this right by the mayor and aldermen of Boston.
3. The date on the poster is April 24, 1851. What is the significance of this date?
The Fugitive Slave Law would have been in effect.

"What's Sauce for the Goose Is Sauce for the Gander"
1. Do you think Edward Williams Clay was for or against the Fugitive Slave Act?
This cartoon mocks the Northerner. Clay was in favor of the Fugitive Slave Act.
2. Explain the meaning of the cartoon's title.
The Southerners in this cartoon adopt the rhetoric of the abolitionists. They apply principles used by Northerners to explain why they will not follow the Fugitive Slave Act to explain why they will not return the Northerner's goods.

Kansas-Nebraska Act
1. How did the passage of this act affect the Missouri Compromise?
The Missouri Compromise, which prohibited slavery in all areas north of 36°30' with the exception of Missouri, was repealed. Now the territories would be allowed to decide for themselves.
2. This act caused a rush into Kansas Territory. Why?
The people living in the territory would vote in order to decide whether or not slavery would be allowed in that territory; therefore, many rushed in to increase the chances for their side to win: pro-slavery or antislavery.

Political Cartoon: "Southern Chivalry"
1. The above political cartoon appeared in a newspaper. Do you think it was a Northern paper or a Southern one?
It appeared in a Northern newspaper. The caption "Southern Chivalry" is sarcastic. It is not really a chivalrous action.
2. In what way did the artist show Sumner in a positive light?
He is holding a pen and paper. These represent "argument" as opposed to "club's" [sic] (violence).
3. In general, what do you think was the point of view of the artist?
Answers will vary, but in general the artist is against his perceived tendency of the Southerners to resort to violence.
4. What do you notice about the Senators in the background?
Some seem to be laughing. None comes to Sumner's assistance.

Dred Scott Decision
1. In your opinion, why did Mrs. Emerson appeal the decision to grant Dred Scott freedom?
Answers will vary. Perhaps it was because slaves were valuable property. Perhaps she wanted to preserve the institution of slavery.
2. How would you describe Dred Scott's actions?
Answers will vary, but two possibilities are *heroic* and *persistent*.
3. On what basis did Dred Scott sue for his freedom?
He believed that because he had lived in a state where slavery was illegal, that he should always be free.
4. On what basis did the Supreme Court rule against him?
The Court's decision concerned whether African-Americans could be considered citizens with the right to sue in federal courts. The Court relied upon historic discrimination to deny African-Americans the rights of citizens. The Court ruled that although they could be citizens of a particular state and could vote in that state, they could not be considered United States citizens because they weren't citizens at the time the Constitution was adopted. Taney reasoned that because they were not citizens, they could not sue in federal court.

The Northern Economy
1. What was the main purpose of this ad? What specific important information did the ad give to customers?
The main purpose of the ad was to tell customers that the railroad was again open for both freight and travel business. Specifically, it told them that the cars and machinery had been replaced and that the bridges and tunnels had been repaired.
2. According to the poster, why did the railroad previously have a good reputation? What past benefit of the route would still be there? What was the new benefit of the route?
The railroad had earned a good reputation because of its speed, security, and comfort. Passengers could still enjoy the beauty of nature along the route. There was now an added historical interest because of the war.

3. Which side controlled the railroad? How do you know?
The Union controlled it. Cleveland, Pittsburgh, Philadelphia, New York, and other Northern cities were being connected.
4. What city could be visited for an extra charge for those passengers going to Baltimore or the Northern Cities?
Travelers could visit Washington City for an extra two dollars.
6. Where did the damage that forced the railroad to close occur? Research to find out who was responsible.
Most occurred "between the Ohio River and Harper's Ferry." Raids by "Stonewall" Jackson and his men were the cause.

Lowell Mills Boarding Houses
1. Read the letter on the next page. When did Mary Paul write it?
She wrote it on December 21, 1845.
2. What did you learn about the working conditions of the mill from reading the letter? Give examples.
Working conditions were very dangerous. She wrote that many lives had been "cut off." One worker broke her neck from a fall on the ice. A man was killed by the cars. Another man broke his ribs. Still another had a bale of cotton fall on him.
3. What portion of Mary's salary went toward her boarding-house rent?
She paid $4.68 for rent out of her $6.60 salary.
4. How many hours a day did Mary typically work?
She worked 11 1/2 hours a day.
5. How did Mary feel about her job?
She seemed content to work there despite the harsh conditions. She liked the girls she worked with and she was proud of the work she did. Also, she said that she would recommend it to other girls looking for employment.
6. Most of the girls who worked in the Lowell Mills were between 15 and 25. How do you think you would feel if you had to live in a company boarding house and work in the mill?
Answers will vary.

The Southern Economy
1. What do you think the women in the photo on the next page are doing? What might the man be doing?
This photo was taken at a plantation in Port Royal Island. The women are preparing the cotton for processing before it is put through the cotton gin. The man is likely supervising their work.
2. Can you guess the function of the house?
The house in the photo was the "gin house." It was where the cotton gin was located.
3. What type of document is shown at the right?
The document is Eli Whitney's patent for his cotton gin. It is dated March 14, 1794.
4. Explain why the cotton gin indirectly led to the increase in slavery even though it made the job of picking out the seeds quicker and less tedious.
It led to an increase in the amount of cotton grown; therefore, more slaves were needed for the large plantations that arose.

Tariffs: "Funeral Obsequies of Free Trade"
1. What is meant by "funeral obsequies"?
It means "funeral rites or services."
2. What is in the coffin?
Free trade is in the coffin.
3. What do the states listed on the grave marker have in common?
These states were against the tariff. The Northern states wanted tariffs on goods imported from other nations. Tariffs made foreign goods more expensive and, therefore, less competitive.
4. Two names on the grave marker are larger than the others. Why?
Opposition in Pennsylvania and New York was especially strong.
5. Alabama, Arkansas, Illinois, Indiana, Louisiana, Michigan, Mississippi, Missouri, South Carolina, Tennessee, and Virginia are missing from the grave marker. Why, do you suppose, did the artist omit them?
The South had little manufacturing of its own and, therefore, Southerners were against tariffs that would lead to higher prices for the goods they needed. The Southern Democrats in these states supported the reduction in tariff rates.
6. Secretary of State Buchanan received criticism for his support of the Walker Tariff. Explain.
Buchanan was from Pennsylvania. He had served in the state legislature as well as the U.S. House of Representatives and the U.S. Senate. He always supported high tariffs. His former constituents were against the lowering of the tariffs.
7. In the lower margin is this statement: "This unfortunate youth died of Home Consumption & was buried at Washington in Nov: 1846." Explain.
The Walker Tariff was passed on that date and in the creator's opinion, free trade—this unfortunate youth—died.

"Slave Auction at Richmond, Virginia"
1. Evaluate the fact that the occasion was referred to as "The Weeping Time."
The name was appropriate. All 436 were born on same plantation, so families and friends would have been broken up, many never to see one another again. They were taken away against their will from the only home they had known.

2. Do you think Crowe was sympathetic to the auctioneer or to the slaves? Explain.

Crowe was sympathetic to the slaves. The phrases "choking sense of horror" and "degrading spectacles" tell us that Crowe was not sympathetic to the auctioneer.

1860 Election of Abraham Lincoln

1. Can you guess what is happening?

It was Lincoln's inauguration on March 4, 1861, as the sixteenth President of the United States.

2. What building is this? Why was there construction?

It is the Capitol Building in Washington, DC. The dome was still under construction. Construction began in 1855 and was not completed until 1866.

"The Political Quadrille, Music by Dred Scott"

1. What is meant by a "quadrille"? If you are not familiar with the word, does the political cartoon give you a clue?

It is a type of square dance.

2. In your opinion, why did the artist place Dred Scott in the center playing the fiddle?

The artist placed Scott in the center to show the importance the Dred Scott Decision would have on the upcoming election. The fact that the candidates are dancing to Scott's music further stresses that importance. The cartoon implies that each candidate's stand on slavery would be a significant factor in the race.

3. Explain the significance of how each of the four candidates was depicted in the cartoon.

The candidates were Abraham Lincoln, John Breckinridge, Stephen Douglas, and John Bell. Each dances with a member of his assumed constituency. Republican candidate Abraham Lincoln (upper right) dances with a black woman, indicating his support of the abolitionists. John Breckinridge, a Southern Democrat, is dancing with President James Buchanan, the Democratic incumbent. Stephen Douglas is dancing with an elderly Irish man, implying his immigrant support. John Bell is dancing with a Native American, probably indicating an interest in Native American interests.

4. Do you notice anything unusual about the way any of the dancers is depicted?

President Buchanan is depicted with the body of a goat, probably because of his nickname, Old Buck.

Secession of 1860 and Fort Sumter

1. What type of document is this? Who sent it? What was its purpose?

It is a telegram. Major Robert Anderson, Union commander at Fort Sumter, sent it. In it he described the evacuation of Fort Sumter and explained the reasons for his retreat.

2. To whom was the document sent and what position did that person hold?

The telegram was sent to Simon Cameron, Secretary of War under President Lincoln.

3. What were the reasons for the evacuation?

The main gates were burned, and the gorge walls were badly damaged. The troops could not get to their arms and ammunition because the doors of the magazine were closed due to the heat effects. They had no provisions except pork.

4. What does the document tell us about the terms of the evacuation?

They were the same terms that had been offered just before the start of the hostilities.

5. Where was the document created?

It was created at sea, on the *S.S. Baltic*.

"The Union Is Dissolved!"

1. What is the name of the newspaper that published this broadside?

The *Charleston Mercury* published it.

2. According to the document, what was repealed and what was the result?

South Carolina's ratification of the Constitution was repealed, and South Carolina was no longer part of the U.S.

3. What purpose do you think broadsides like this served?

They served to spread news to the people—in this case, the news that the Union had dissolved.

Jefferson Davis

1. Entitled "Jeff Davis Reaping the Harvest," this print was created for the October 26, 1861, issue of *Harper's Weekly*. What is Jefferson Davis doing in the print?

He is reaping stalks, which have small skulls on the top.

2. Describe the mood that is created by this print. What elements help create that mood?

It is very dark, spooky, and macabre. Contributing factors are Davis's eyes, the skulls, the vulture, the snake, and the noose. Davis is portrayed as the "grim reaper."

3. In your opinion, which side did the creator of the print blame for the loss of life caused by the Civil War?

It would seem as if the creator believed the Confederates were to blame.

The First Battle of Bull Run (Manassas)

1. What event is depicted in the above illustration?

The illustration depicts the Union retreat after the First Battle of Bull Run (Manassas).

2. Describe the scene depicted in the above illustration.

There is panic and general confusion. Wagons are overturned. Horses have fallen or are out of control. Several people are lying on the ground; some appear dead or injured. Others seem to be running to get away. Crowds of people are seen in the background.

3. What appears to be the main cause of the chaos?

The wagons carrying spectators are jamming the path.

4. Which side is retreating? How do you know (in addition to the writing below the image)?

The Union is retreating. They are carrying the Union flag.

5. Why, do you think, did the artist include "Sunday Afternoon" in the title?

Many came to witness the event wrongly thinking they would spend a pleasant Sunday afternoon picnicking and enjoying the excitement.

Spying on the Enemy

1. To whom did the words "our President" in the notes refer?

They referred to Jefferson Davis, President of the Confederacy.

2. To what debt did the note refer? How do you know?

It referred to the information delivered to General Beauregard that helped the Confederates win the First Battle of Bull Run. We know because of the date: July 22, 1861.

3. This coded letter, written on mourning paper, was used by "Rebel Rose." Can you guess how experts know it was mourning paper? Why might she have used it? What would have been needed to decode the letter?

The black border shows it was mourning paper. It may have made it easier to deceive someone who saw it. A cipher code would have been needed to decode it.

Ironclads: Battle of the *Monitor* and the *Merrimac*

Lithograph

1. Which is the *Monitor* and which is the *Merrimac?* How do you know?

The *Monitor* is the one on the bottom left. It has the flag of the United States. The *Merrimac* has the Confederate flag. Also, if you look closely, you can see that the *Merrimac* has more guns.

2. Do you think the creator of the lithograph was pro-Union or pro-Confederate? What makes you think that?

Most will probably say that the creator was pro-Union. The battle was inconclusive, yet the creator chose to write that the *Monitor* "whipped" the *Merrimac* and other vessels. The creator referred to the *Monitor* as "little *Monitor.*" The creator said there was a whole "School" of Rebel Steamers, which makes it seem as if the Confederates should have won. Currier & Ives was located in New York, so it is likely that most of its support came from the North.

3. Research and report on other technological advancements that affected the military during the Civil War. Which side benefitted the most and why?

Answers will vary, but among the advances were torpedoes, submarines, repeating rifles, Minié bullets (type of bullet for muzzle-loading rifles), hot-air balloons, expanded use of the telegraph, and railroads. The North benefitted the most from the improvement in weaponry because they had the factories and the manufacturing experience. They also benefitted the most from the railroads. At the start of the war, the North had more than twice the length of railroad tracks. Also, because their tracks were more standardized, they could more easily use the rails to move troops and supplies.

4. What do you see in the background?

You can see people watching the battle from the decks of the ships and along the shore.

Letter

1. What does the letter describe?

It describes the naval clashes that took place on March 8 and 9, 1862.

2. Who wrote the letter and who were the recipients?

Major-General Benjamin Huger wrote the letter to S.R. Mallory, Secretary of the Navy. He sent a copy to General S. Cooper, Adjutant and Inspector General.

3. On which side were the sender and the recipients? How do you know?

They were Confederates. The author was not sure that the *Monitor* was the correct name: "…would probably have been destroyed but for the ironclad battery of the enemy called, I think, the *Monitor.*" Also, he wrote that the enemy could build the ships faster than they could. He wrote the following: "At present, in the *Virginia;* we have the advantage…."

4. What were the author's conclusions?

The author concluded that only ironclads could beat other ironclads. Although he thought the South had the current advantage, he believed that would change because the North had the advantage building new ships.

West Virginia

1. Underline the sentence in Article IV, Section 3, of the U.S. Constitution that explains why West Virginia had to secede from Virginia before it could enter the Union as a new state.

Article IV, Section 3. New states may be admitted by the Congress into this union; but no new states shall be formed or erected within the jurisdiction of any other state; nor any state be formed by the junction of two or more states, or parts of states, without the consent of the legislatures of the states concerned as well as of the Congress.

2. When Section 1 of the ordinance was read, several delegates wanted a change. Read the introduction of the section and the excerpts of two delegates' (Sinsel and Brown) views.... Briefly explain each point of view.

Harmon Sinsel of Taylor County made a motion to strike the word "Kanawha" in the first section. He said that he was raised a Virginian and was proud to be one. He also referred to the fact that it was in honor of the Virgin Queen and also made him think of the Virgin Mary.

William G. Brown of Kanawha County had a different point of view. He believed the delegates should keep the name "Kanawha" because it was the name in the ordinance that the people had voted on. "That ordinance prescribes definitely the name of the State proposed to be erected...."

3. Daniel Lamb of Wheeling objected to any form of the name Virginia. He was angered by the way the eastern part of the state treated the western part of the state. Why did the eastern region have more power?

The eastern part of the state was much more populous, so it had more delegates. Those delegates passed laws that helped those living in eastern Virginia without considering the needs of those living in the western part of the state.

4. The 1862 map above shows the proposed state of Kanawha. It is from Frank Leslie's *Pictorial History of the American Civil War*, 1862. Study the map and use geographic features to explain why many in the western part of the state favored separation.

The mountains separated the western portion of Virginia from the rest of the state. It was easier for those living in western Virginia to get to Ohio and Pennsylvania than it was to get to the eastern part of Virginia. This was true not only by roads but also by rivers. The largest city in the western part of the state was Wheeling. Wheeling is only 50 miles from Pittsburgh, Pennsylvania, but 330 miles to Richmond, Virginia. It is not surprising that the people of West Virginia identified more with those living in neighboring states than with those in the eastern part of Virginia.

Antietam

1. How might Alexander Gardner's photographs have changed people's views of the war?

Answers will vary, but at the start of the war many people held idealistic views. They believed it would be short and they did not envision the slaughter. These and similar photos documented the horrors of war. Viewers could see the slaughter that was occurring. They could see the bodies strewn throughout the countryside. Because it was often possible to see their faces, many could recognize the victims.

2. Describe the mood evoked by these photos. How do you think these and similar photos made the viewers feel?

The mood was one of horror. They could see the result of brothers fighting against brothers. It probably made the horrors of war seem more real to them. It likely both frightened and saddened them.

3. Look at the top photo. What did people learn about the way the fallen soldiers were buried?

They learned that they were buried in trenches.

Letters

From Alexander Hunter

1. Was the writer of this letter on the Confederate or Union side? How do you know?

The writer was a Confederate. "It was the first ragged Rebels" the people lining the roads had seen. Also, they were singing "Maryland, My Maryland," which was popular with the Confederates.

2. Describe their diet while camped in the apple orchard.

Their diet comprised apples and corn in many forms.

3. Describe the general condition of the men. What happened to the men who could not keep up?

They were sick and hungry. Many were lame. Their clothing was dirty and torn. Their socks were worn. Many had no shoes. Those who couldn't keep up, were left on the road.

4. How did the farmers they passed treat the soldiers? Why were the farmers relieved?

They treated them well and gave generously. The farmers were relieved that their property was not destroyed. The soldiers did not enter their homes and did not harm their property.

5. How would you have felt if you were Alexander Hunter's family receiving this letter?

Answers will vary, but they were likely ambivalent. They were probably relieved that he was alive but saddened and frightened by the conditions.

From J.O. Smith

6. What prompted J.O. Smith to write this letter?

J.O. Smith, the writer of the letter, witnessed a Confederate soldier carrying a Union soldier on his shoulders and joined the crowd following them.

7. How did the Yank and the Reb cooperate with one another?
The Reb rode the horse and carried the wounded Yank; the Yank gave directions to the field hospital as they travelled.
8. The home of William and Margaret Roulette was used after the battle as a field hospital for Union soldiers. Why did the people in the field hospital cry for help as strongly for the Reb as for the Yank as they entered the hospital?
The Reb had been blinded, but he carried the wounded Yank on his shoulders so that he, too, could be helped.

Clara Barton
1. What was the purpose of her letter?
Clara Barton wanted the President to authorize her to carry on an official writing campaign in which she would request information from or give information to family members and friends of the missing.
2. Describe Miss Barton's handwriting. Why, do you think, did she write in this style?
Answers will vary, but she might have wanted to get President Lincoln's attention by having her letter stand out among the many he received. Perhaps she wanted to stress the importance that she attached to her request.
3. Clara Barton said … in reference to her experience in Antietam. Rewrite the quotation in your own words.
Answers will vary,

Emancipation Proclamation
1. Read the opening paragraph of the Preliminary Emancipation Proclamation (shown above). What did President Lincoln cite as the reason for the war?
The original objective, which remained, was to restore the Union.
2. What new objective of the war was described?
The new objective was the abolition of slavery.
3. What will happen on January 1, 1863?
Slaves in states that are in rebellion against the United States will be freed.
4. How will the President determine which states are not in rebellion against the United States?
The fact that a state is represented in Congress will be evidence it is not in rebellion.
5. What did the President ask of the newly freed slaves?
He asked that they refrain from violence except in self-defense and that they try to get a job for reasonable wages.
6. What did the document say about the newly freed slaves and the military?
The document said that the newly freed slaves would be welcomed into the armed services of the United States.

"Emancipation" by Thomas Nast
1. What, do you think, prompted Nast to change the image in the bottom circle?
It was probably Lincoln's assassination. Lincoln had become a martyr and was often referred to as the Great Emancipator.
2. Above the large center circle is an illustration of Thomas Crawford's statue entitled "Freedom." How would you describe the scene inside the large center circle? What is the mood created by that scene?
It is a family scene. The scene is very tranquil. The family seems to be content. An example is the father bouncing the child on his knee. They are gathered around a stove that has the word "Union" printed on it. There is a picture of Lincoln hanging next to a banjo on the wall. All of this creates a happy mood and optimism about the future.
3. Nast contrasted the lives of the slaves under the Confederacy with what would hopefully be their future lives as free men and women. Cite examples of the evils of slavery shown on the left half of the illustration.
The following scenes depict the evils of slavery: fugitive slaves are being hunted in a swamp, a black man is being sold and separated from his wife and children, a black woman is flogged, and a black male is branded.
4. Cite examples of what Nast predicted would be their lives as free men and women shown on the right.
The following are scenes that depict the future: a cottage in peaceful surroundings, a black mother sending her children off to public school, and a black man receiving pay for work done.
5. Contrast the image over the scenes on the left with the image over the scenes on the right.
Above the scenes on the left is the three-headed Cerberus, a creature called the "Hound of Hades" in Greek mythology. It is frightening and evokes a feeling of danger. Above the scenes on the right is a woman with an olive branch, a symbol of peace. It is reassuring and evokes a feeling of calmness and tranquility.
6. Contrast the images on either side of the small circle.
In the image on the left the overseer is flogging a slave. It represents the harsh past. The image on the right is more optimistic about the future. In it the foreman is greeting the field workers.

Recruitment Posters: "To Arms! To Arms!"
1. Is this a Union or a Confederate recruitment poster? Who is doing the recruiting? According to the poster, why should men enlist with this volunteer company instead of waiting to get drafted?
It is a Confederate poster. Captain Stickleman's Company Virginia Volunteers is doing the recruiting. According to the poster this company can offer better benefits.
2. How many recruits are needed?
Sixty recruits are needed.

© **Barbara M. Peller**

3. The poster says that the recruit will receive a bounty of 50 dollars. Explain what that means.
The recruit will receive a bonus of $50 upon being enrolled.
4. What other money will the recruit receive upon being enrolled? Do we know what the monthly pay will be?
He will receive $25 for clothing. No, we do not know the monthly pay.
5. What must happen before a recruit can be officially enrolled?
He has to be examined and—it can be inferred—okayed by an Army Surgeon.
6. Where should a man go if he is interested in joining the company?
He should go to one of the public meetings listed at the bottom of the poster.
7. What do you think the recruiters thought was the best enticement? What makes you think that?
They probably thought $50 bounty was the best enticement because it was in the largest and boldest print.

Recruitment Posters: "Cavalry to the Field!"
1. According to the "Cavalry to the Field!" poster, what was the range of pay if a recruit joined the 1st Battalion N.Y. Mounted Rifles?
The range of pay was from $13 to $23 per month.
2. Why was the 1st Battalion N.Y. Mounted Rifles seeking recruits? How many were wanted?
The battalion was seeking 20 recruits because the Secretary of War had ordered that the battalion be increased to a regiment.
3. What adjective did the Secretary of War use to describe the battalion?
He used the adjective "efficient."
4. What could each recruit expect to receive after he enlisted? Upon reaching the regiment? Upon being mustered in?
Each recruit could expect to be paid $4 after enlistment, a month's pay when reaching the regiment, and $40 from the state upon being mustered in.
5. Use context clues to define the verb "muster." Look up the definition if you are not sure.
Muster means to assemble (troops), especially for inspection or in preparation for battle.
6. Were any patriotic symbols used?
Yes, the United States flag was shown in the background.
7. Do you think this recruitment poster was an effective enticement? Explain your point of view.
Answers will vary, but some might think the officer on horseback with his sword drawn is exciting.

Black Soldiers in the Civil War
1. What was the main purpose of this poster?
The main purpose was to encourage black men to enlist in the Union Army for 3 years of service.
2. The broadside says that race relations had changed. What was the reason for that change?
Lincoln had issued the Emancipation Proclamation.
3. Cite some reasons given why blacks should enlist.
The following reasons were given: They must show they are worthy to be freemen. Their enemies have portrayed them as cowards, and they must prove them wrong. They should make sure they do not leave their children "an inheritance of shame." They must show that they are equal to "Englishmen, Irishmen, White Americans, and other Races" in their humanity.
4. Which two incidents of valor shown by men of color did the recruitment poster cite? Research these incidents and summarize their significance.
Port Hudson: The last Union engagement to recapture the Mississippi River was the siege of Port Hudson, Louisiana. The 1st Louisiana Native Guard was an early all-black regiment. This regiment was crucial in the success of the campaign. It comprised some free men of color from New Orleans, but most were escaped slaves.
Milliken's Bend: This was a small battle in the Vicksburg Campaign. Black Union soldiers distinguished themselves in spite of the fact that they had little military training and inferior weapons.
5. Of all the reasons given, which do you think was most convincing? Can you think of any other reasons that might have been included?
Answers will vary.

The Siege of Vicksburg
1. Locate Vicksburg, Mississippi, on a map. Use its location to explain its strategic importance.
Vicksburg is on the east bank of the Mississippi River. It is about halfway between Memphis and New Orleans, two important Confederate cities. Control of the river and the railroad prevented the Confederates from getting reinforcements and supplies. The siege of Vicksburg virtually cut the Confederacy in two.
2. Read the July 13, 1863, letter from President Lincoln to Ulysses S. Grant. What are the main reasons for the letter?
The President wanted to congratulate Grant and to express his gratitude for what Grant did for his country with his successful siege of Vicksburg. He also wanted to acknowledge that he had doubted his strategy but that Grant had been right and he had been wrong.

3. What does this letter tell you about President Lincoln?
Answers may vary, but some may say it shows that Lincoln had enough humility and enough self-confidence to admit when he was wrong. It also shows that he took an interest in the individual campaigns but was smart enough to let those with more experience in those matters make decisions when appropriate.

The Battle of Gettysburg
1. Read the letter on the next page. In Lincoln's view, what would have happened if General Meade had pursued General Lee?
Lincoln believed that "to have closed upon him would, in connection with the our other late successes, have ended the war." In other words, the war would have ended sooner.
2. Lincoln later replaced Meade as Commander of the Army of the Potomac with General Ulysses S. Grant. Find an excerpt from the letter that might explain his reasoning.
The following might explain it: "If you could not safely attack Lee last Monday, how can you possibly do so South of the river, when you can take with you very few more then two thirds of the force you then had in hand?"
3. Have you ever written a letter to express your anger and then not sent it? If so, did venting your emotions change the way you felt? If you have not done this yourself, evaluate how effective you think this would be.
Answers will vary.

The Gettysburg Address
1. Read the transcriptions of the Nicolay and Bliss copies. What is the most significant change?
Lincoln added the words "under God."
2. Summarize the main reason for the gathering.
They had gathered to dedicate the portion of the battlefield that had been established as a cemetery for the Union soldiers who had died during the Battle of Gettysburg.
3. Were both Union and Confederate soldiers being buried in the Soldiers' National Cemetery? How do you know?
The speech says that it is "a final resting place for those who died here, that the nation might live."
4. What was the "great task" Lincoln referred to?
The task was the restoration of the Union so that the fallen soldiers would not have died in vain.
5. Some words were taken from another important American document. Explain.
The opening sentence contains words from the Declaration of Independence: "all men are created equal."
6. Look up the definition of any word you are unsure of.... Rewrite the speech in your own words.
Answers will vary.
7. Why, do you think, did Lincoln underline the word "did" in the sentence beginning "The world will little note"?
He wanted to emphasize that the soldiers who had died in battle should be remembered. He believed that what they *did* was more important than what he *said*.
8. Many people believe that presenting things in threes can make a speech more effective. Find examples of President Lincoln's use of the "Rule of Three" when writing this speech.
These are examples: we can not dedicate—we can not consecrate—we can not hallow; little note, nor long remember ..., but it can never forget; and of the people, by the people, for the people.
9. According to Lincoln, what was the job of the living?
Lincoln believed it was the job of the living to dedicate themselves to the cause for which the fallen soldiers had died—the preservation of the Union.

The Election of 1864: "The True Issue or 'That's What's the Matter' "
1. What are Lincoln and Davis pulling on?
They are pulling on a map of the United States.
2. What is happening to the object they are pulling on as a result?
The map, which represents the United States, is tearing apart.
3. Who is saying what?
McClellan: "The Union must be preserved at all hazards!"
Lincoln: "No peace without abolition."
Davis: "No peace without Separation!!"
4. How is McClellan portrayed? What does that tell us about what McClellan might have done to end the war if he had won the election?
McClellan believed that preserving the Union was of primary importance. He is shown as an intermediary between the two opposing forces, inferring that he might have compromised with the Confederacy to keep the Union together.

The Election of 1864: "The Grand, National Union Banner for 1864"
1. What type of poster is this?
It is a campaign poster for the Election of 1864.

2. Why are Abraham Lincoln and Andrew Johnson featured on the poster?
Lincoln's running mate for his second term was Andrew Johnson. They ran on the National Union Party ticket. This was a temporary name during the war. Only states that remained in the Union took part in the election.

3. What feelings is the poster meant to evoke? What images help evoke those feelings?
The poster is meant to evoke feelings of patriotism: The "Temple of Liberty" has two American flags on each side. A female figure holds a staff and liberty cap. An eagle with spread wings holds a banner in its mouth and arrows in its talons. Rays of light ending in stars emanate from the temple. It is also meant to evoke feelings of peace and prosperity: Below the portraits a man is plowing a field. Farm buildings are in the background. Cornucopias on either side spill over with fruit.

General Sherman's March to the Sea

1. In the engraving on the following page, you can see two of the men trying to take down a telegraph pole. Why, do you suppose, would they want to do that?
Sherman wanted to keep their plans as secret as possible. He did not want anyone to be able to spread the news of what was occurring or to tell which way they were heading.

2. Look at the portion of the engraving shown at the top of the next page. What are the men in the bottom right corner doing? Why, do you suppose, would they want to do that?
They are making the railroad tracks unusable. This would prevent the Confederates from moving men and supplies.

3. In general, why did Sherman order the destruction of bridges, railroads, and tunnels?
The loss of these structures made it more difficult to wage war.

4. In general, why did he order the men to burn the houses and barns?
Sherman wanted to destroy the will of the Confederate civilians to continue the war.

5. Evaluate the success of Sherman's destruction of military targets; infrastructure, such as bridges and tunnels; and civilian property.
Sherman damaged the economy and transportation of the Confederates. It probably led to an earlier surrender and end to the war. Although often thought of as a brute, Sherman believed his method of destroying property was better than having many more casualties.

Letter from President Lincoln to General Sherman

1. What, do you think, was the main idea of Sherman's letter to Lincoln?
Sherman's December 22 letter presented Savannah to the President as a Christmas gift.

2. Why didn't President Lincoln tell Sherman of his apprehensions when Sherman set out for Savannah?
Lincoln believed that Sherman was the better judge in these matters. He also believed "nothing risked, nothing gained."

3. Whom did President Lincoln credit for the success of the campaign? What does it tell us about the President?
Lincoln credited General Sherman and also General Thomas. This shows that President Lincoln was willing to give credit to others when deserved. Also, it shows that he valued their expertise and strategic abilities.

4. How else did Lincoln show that he had faith in his generals?
Lincoln said that he would leave it up to General Grant and General Sherman to decide what would come next.

Mary Edwards Walker

1. What do you notice about the way Dr. Walker sometimes dressed? In your opinion, why did she dress this way?
She sometimes wore men's clothing. (This type of clothing was unusual for women of that time period.) Answers will vary, but men's clothing was less restrictive and more practical for the duties she had to perform. As an advocate for women's rights, she also might have been making a statement.

2. Evaluate President Carter's decision to restore the medals to Dr. Walker and the others.
Answers will vary, but most will probably agree that they deserved the awards.

"The Campaign in Virginia—On to Richmond"

1. General Grant is in the illustration. Can you identify him?
Grant is on horseback.

2. What is the mood created by this illustration?
The mood is inspirational. Although some of the men have fallen, they have not given up. Many have their swords raised. The soldier in the foreground is seen waving the others on even though he has fallen. We can feel the onward motion of the men.

3. *Harper's Weekly,* which was published in New York, favored the Union side during the Civil War. How do you think its readers reacted to this picture?
Answers will vary, but the determined look of the Union soldiers may have given them some optimism that victory was possible.

The Fall of Richmond

1. Describe the scene in the lithograph entitled "Fall of Richmond."

The scene is the evacuation of the Confederate soldiers and the citizens on horseback, in carriages, and on foot. They are crossing the Mayo Bridge over the James River on the night of April 2, 1865. There are several fires.

2. Identify the columned building located to the right of the fires.

The Virginia Capitol Building, being used as the Confederate Capitol, is seen to the right of the fires.

3. Describe the scene in the bottom visual on the previous page. What can we learn about the columned building identified in Number 2 above?

There is a great deal of destruction following the fires started by the Confederates before evacuating the city. Although there is destruction nearby, the Capitol remained unharmed.

4. What can we infer from the photo below?

The retreating Confederate soldiers were under orders to set fire to bridges, the armory, and supply warehouses as they left. We can infer that they burned the Mayo Bridge over the James River after crossing it.

Surrender at Appomattox Court House

1. Compare the demeanors of Grant and Lee. Cite reasons for your opinion.

Lee's demeanor is somber, stiff, formal, and dignified. Grant appears much more casual and relaxed. Grant's shoulders are relaxed. He is sitting a little sideways. His arms are casually sitting in his lap. His legs are crossed. Lee is sitting straight. His arms are stiffly placed on the arm rests. His legs are straight in front of him.

2. The agreement between General Grant and General Lee is often referred to as a "Gentlemen's Agreement." Evaluate the appropriateness of that term.

Answers will vary, but most people think the terms were very fair. Lee and his men were treated with respect.

Andersonville Prison

1. Describe what you see in the top photo.

There is extreme overcrowding. The men seem to be waiting for something.

2. Can you guess what is happening?

The men in the foreground are handing out rations to the men.

3. The photo on the bottom is the southwest view of stockade. Describe what you see.

These are the makeshift tents that the prisoners slept in. The fence is the "dead line" that the prisoners could not cross. If they attempted to cross, they would likely be shot.

The Assassination of President Lincoln

1. Explain the purpose of this document.

It was to offer a reward for information leading to the capture of Booth and two of his accomplices.

2. Why, do you think, did Booth believe that killing Johnson and Seward would throw the government into disarray?

They were the next two in line for succession to become President if the President died.

3. Who are the three people shown at the top?

In the center is John Wilkes Booth, who assassinated President Lincoln. The others were two of his accomplices: On the left is John Surratt (son of Mary Surratt). On the right is David Herold, who guided Powell to the home of Secretary Seward (see #7 below). **Note of Interest:** Unlike the other eight conspirators, who were convicted, John Surratt's trial ended in a mistrial, and he was not punished. Four of those convicted were hanged.

4. Who was offering the reward? What was the breakdown of the $100,000 being offered?

The War Department offered the reward. The breakdown was $50,000 for Booth and $25,000 each for Surratt and Herold.

5. Research and find out why the attempted assassination of the Secretary of State was mentioned on the poster but not that of the Vice President.

Lewis T. Powell carried out his instructions and burst into Secretary of State Seward's home. He shot and wounded the secretary and three others. George A. Atzerodt lost his nerve and did not attack the Vice President.

6. According to the poster, what will be the punishment for the murderer and his accomplices if found guilty by the Military Commission?

Punishment will be death.

7. According to the poster, how could the pain caused by the President's assassination be alleviated?

The arrest and punishment of the guilty parties would alleviate the pain: "Let the stain of innocent blood be removed from the land by the arrest and punishment of the murderers."

8. What is at the bottom of the poster following Stanton's name and title?

There is a description of the three men. There is also a notice of additional rewards.

Civil War Music
"The Songs of War"
1. See if you can figure out which song is represented by each scene.
Top: The scene at the left shows a drummer boy motivating the troops in battle; it represents "The Bold Soldier Boy." The scene to the right of that shows George McClellan on horseback; he had been appointed General in Chief of the Union Armies in the same month the print was published; it represents the song "Hail to the Chief." The two scenes to the right show that camp life could be rowdy. In the first, a man is seen drinking out of a canteen, and a fight has broken out behind him; this scene represents "We'll Be Free and Easy Still." The second shows men being taken out of camp; it is linked to "Rogue's March." (Possibly following "We'll Be Free and Easy Still" to show the consequences of drinking.)
Bottom: Soldiers are marching and singing; this scene represents "Battle Hymn of the Republic." To the right an African-American is sitting on a barrel; it is difficult to see, but the barrel is marked "Contraband" to show that he is an ex-slave. This scene represents "Dixie."
Center: The image of the woman in the center stands for loved ones left behind; it represents "The Girl I Left Behind."
2. "Dixie" was a battle cry of the South. Why, do you think, did Winslow Homer include it?
Although "Dixie" was a battle cry for the South, it was created in the North as a minstrel song and remained popular there. Answers may vary, but he may have included it with that visual as a reminder of why they were fighting.

"Grafted into the Army"
1. Explain the pun on which this song is based.
The play on words is the use of "*grafted* into the army" instead of "*drafted* into the army."
2. Why did many people protest these acts?
The rich were able to get out of the draft, either by paying someone to take their place or by paying the exemption fee.
3. Summarize the story told by this song.
The song tells the story of a woman who is upset that her youngest son has been drafted. It seems like just yesterday that she was holding him on her lap, and now he is being sent to war. She had hoped that because she was a widow and because her other sons had died in the war, they would not take him, but they did. She is afraid he, too, will die.
4. What is the woman on the cover of the sheet music holding in her hand? What does the image on the bottom represent?
She is holding a pair of torn trousers that her son wore as a child. The image below is of a young soldier walking picket duty; he represents the woman's son who has been drafted into the army.

"The Bonnie Blue Flag," *by Harry McCarthy*
1. Read the lyrics found on page 92 and describe in one sentence the story told by the song.
The song recounts the secession of the states that became the Confederacy one by one in order of their secession.
2. General Butler, who ruled over New Orleans when the Union occupied the city, issued an order (General Order No. 40) that made singing or owning the song "The Bonnie Blue Flag" an act of treason. Use the definition of treason as stated in Article III, Section 3, of the Constitution to evaluate that order.
Answers will vary, but the following is the definition according to that section: "Treason against the United States, shall consist only in levying War against them, or in adhering to their Enemies, giving them Aid and Comfort. ..."

"Tramp, Tramp, Tramp," *by George F. Root*
1. Read the lyrics of "Tramp, Tramp, Tramp" found on page 90. From whose point of view is it written.
It is written from the point of view of a prisoner of war waiting to be freed.

Reconstruction Amendments
1. What do the three Reconstruction Amendments have in common?
The amendments abolished slavery and guaranteed equal protection of the laws and the right to vote.
2. Create a one-sentence summary for each of the three amendments.
The Thirteenth Amendment abolished slavery. The Fourteenth Amendment guaranteed U.S. citizenship to all persons born or naturalized in the United States and granted them federal civil rights. The Fifteenth Amendment decreed that the right to vote could not be denied because of "race, color, or previous condition of servitude."
3. A portion of the Fourteenth Amendment was later changed by the Twenty-sixth Amendment. Explain.
The Twenty-sixth Amendment lowered the voting age from 21 to 18 in both state and federal elections.

Cartoon Analysis Worksheet

Level 1

Visuals	Words (not all cartoons include words)
1. List the objects or people you see in the cartoon.	1. Identify the cartoon caption and/or title.
	2. Locate three words or phrases used by the cartoonist to identify objects or people within the cartoon.
	3. Record any important dates or numbers that appear in the cartoon.

Level 2

Visuals	Words
2. Which of the objects on your list are symbols?	4. Which words or phrases in the cartoon appear to be the most significant? Why do you think so?
3. What do you think each symbol means?	5. List adjectives that describe the emotions portrayed in the cartoon.

Level 3

A. Describe the action taking place in the cartoon.

B. Explain how the words in the cartoon clarify the symbols.

C. Explain the message of the cartoon.

D. What special interest groups would agree/disagree with the cartoon's message? Why?

**Designed and developed by the
Education Staff, National Archives and Records Administration,
Washington, DC 20408**

Photo Analysis Worksheet

Step 1. Observation

A.	Study the photograph for 2 minutes. Form an overall impression of the photograph and then examine individual items. Next, divide the photo into quadrantes an study each section to see what new details become visible.
B.	Use the chart below to list people, objects, and activities in the photograph.

People	Objects	Activities

Step 2. Inference

Based on what you have observed above, list three things you might infer from this photograph.

Step 3. Questions

A.	What questions does this photograph raise in your mind?
B.	Where could you find answers to them?

**Designed and developed by the
Education Staff, National Archives and Records Administration,
Washington, DC 20408**

Written Document Analysis Worksheet

1.	TYPE OF DOCUMENT (Check one):		
	○ Newspaper	○ Map	○ Advertisement
	○ Letter	○ Telegram	○ Congressional Record
	○ Patent	○ Press Release	○ Census Report
	○ Memorandum	○ Report	○ Other

2.	UNIQUE PHYSICAL CHARACTERISTICS OF THE DOCUMENT (Check one or more):	
	☐ Interesting Letterhead	☐ Notations
	☐ Handwritten	☐ "RECEIVED" stamp
	☐ Typed	☐ Other
	☐ Seals	

3. DATE(S) OF DOCUMENT:

4. AUTHOR (OR CREATOR) OF THE DOCUMENT:

POSITION (TITLE):

5. FOR WHAT AUDIENCE WAS THE DOCUMENT WRITTEN?

6. DOCUMENT INFORMATION (There are many possible ways to answer A-E.)

A. List three things the author said that you think are important:

B. Why do you think this document was written?

C. What evidence in the document helps you know why it was written? Quote from the document.

D. List two things the document tells you about life in the United States at the time it was written.

E. Write a question to the author that is left unanswered by the document:

Designed and developed by the
Education Staff, National Archives and Records Administration,
Washington, DC 20408

CPSIA information can be obtained
at www.ICGtesting.com
Printed in the USA
LVHW051716281019
635543LV00004B/1946

9 781566 446167